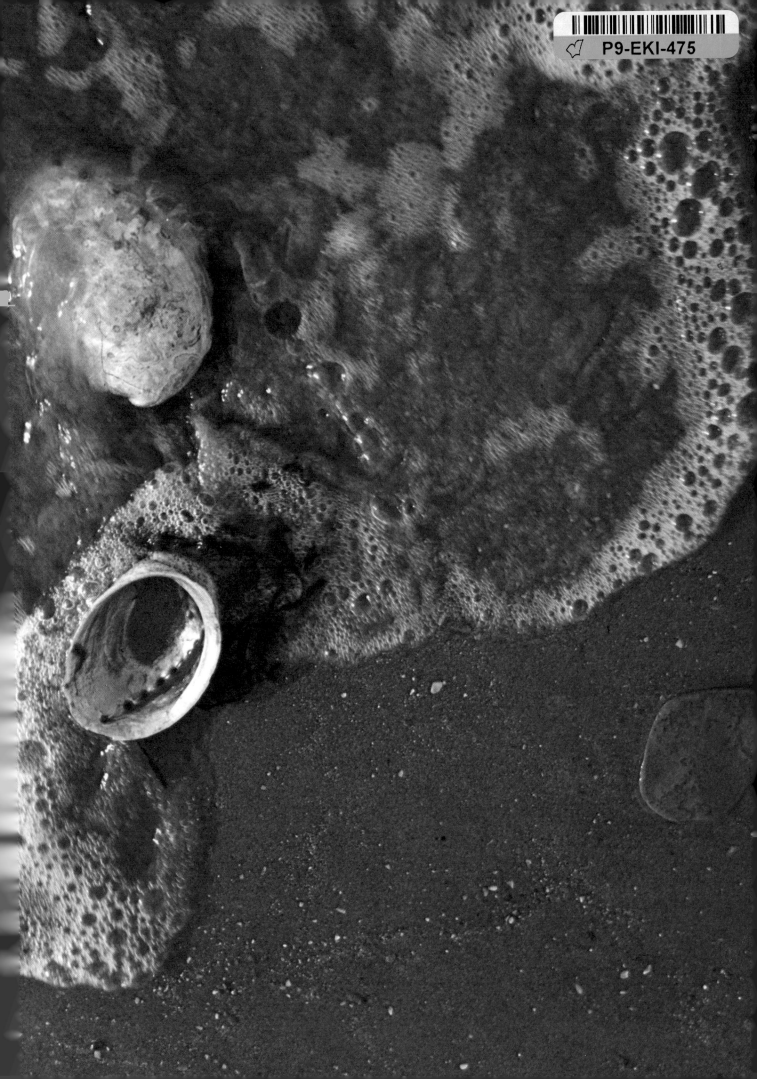

all color book of
seashells

by JM Clayton

CHARTWELL
BOOKS, INC.

This book originally published in
Great Britain in 1972 by
Octopus Books Ltd

This 1989 edition
published by
Chartwell Books, Inc.
A Division of Book Sales Inc.
110 Enterprise Avenue
Secaucus
New Jersey 07094

© 1974 Octopus Books Ltd

ISBN 1-55521-361-8

Produced by Mandarin Offset
Printed in Hong Kong

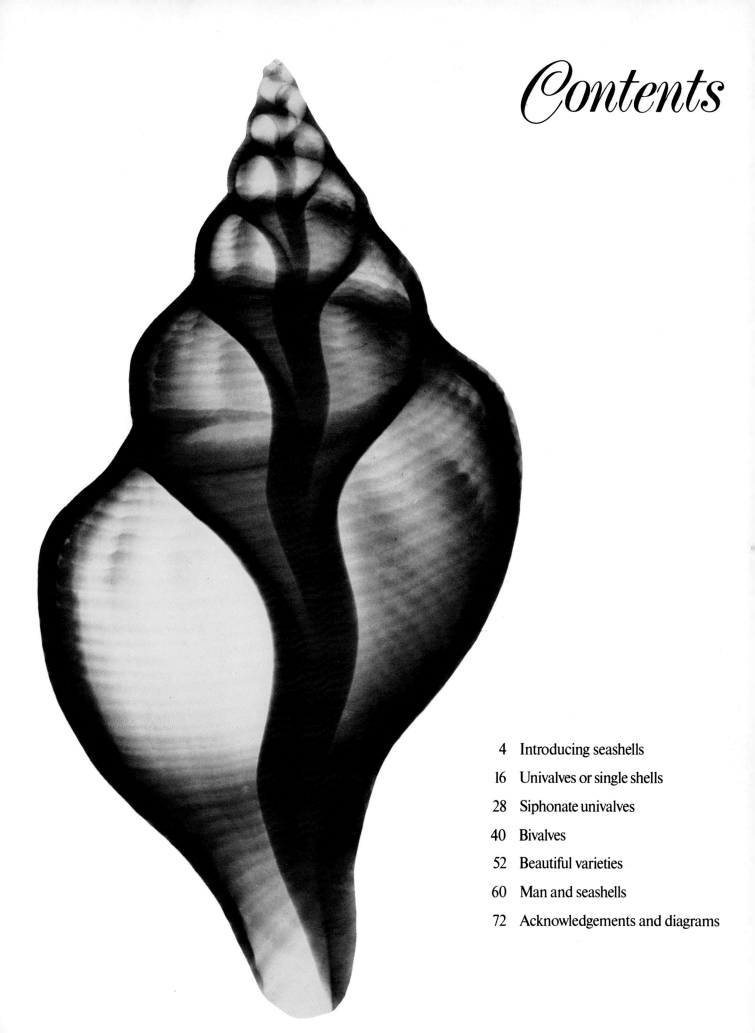

Contents

Right
This is a beautifully sculptured and brightly coloured large gastropod which lives in tropical waters. A spider conch has such an unusual shape that is easy to recognize and the different species can be readily identified by the number and form of the spines. This orange spider conch, *Lambis crocata*, grows to a length of approximately 10 cm.

Far right
The common or edible whelk *Buccinum undatum* is a good example of a gastropod shell with a siphonal groove and the siphon can be clearly seen, as can the large foot used in crawling over the ocean floor and the distinct head, bearing tentacles. The pink and green patches on the shell are algal growths and the white line is the limy tube of a polychaete worm. This species is common offshore in the North Atlantic and can grow to a length of 7.5 cm.

Introducing seashells

Seashells are some of nature's most beautiful works of art and few people who wander along the beach, whether young or old, can resist picking up the shells they find.

Although seashells are inanimate they are produced by living animals for protection of the soft body, remaining intact long after the owner has died. These shell-secreting animals belong to the large group of phylum called Mollusca, and some of its members are found in all seas of the world. Therefore any beach can be the starting point for the would-be shell-collector but, needless to say, some shores support much larger molluscan populations than others and information on the most suitable beaches is best obtained from shell books pertaining to local areas.

The greatest pleasure and satisfaction in this hobby comes from finding out about the life of the animals as well as collecting the lovely shells and many happy hours can be spent searching for and watching the habits of the living molluscs in their natural surroundings. Rocky or coral shores are the most rewarding as these have many cracks, crevices, loose stones, covering vegetation and pools where the animals shelter for protection when the tide ebbs. When vegetation is displaced or rocks turned over in the search *always* put them back as found so that all the creatures are returned to their original protected positions, otherwise there will be many unnecessary deaths. Much fun can be had in searching the debris of the driftline, particularly after a period of strong onshore winds when the rough seas are beginning to subside. Often many of the molluscs living in deeper water are stranded on the beach and besides an abundance of empty shells some still containing the occupants can often be found.

Whenever possible collect empty shells or shells containing dead animals, but when it is necessary to collect live specimens limit the number taken to the bare minimum for your needs. Wanton removal of live animals by many collectors may soon deplete the breeding populations and eventually lead to the extinction of some species in certain areas. With more and more people following this exciting hobby, it is ever important to bear this in mind, otherwise in a few years the now richly populated shores will have little to offer future collectors.

The **Mollusca** are invertebrates which have a special extension of the body wall, called the mantle. This has certain cells able to secrete an outer protective covering called the exoskeleton and known to everyone as the shell.

The shell appears to consist of one substance but, in fact, it has three layers. The outer layer is a thin, horny covering, called the periostracum, which is composed of the organic substance conchiolin (often abbreviated to conchin). The middle layer is the hard, chalky region of the shell, formed basically of calcium carbonate. Both of these layers are secreted by cells at the edge of the mantle; this means that the youngest material is always at the outside edge of the shell next to the mantle. The innermost layer, also formed principally of calcium carbonate, is secreted by cells over the whole surface of the mantle. Although both the innermost and middle layers are formed of calcium carbonate, they have quite different crystalline forms; those of the middle layer are prismatic, which means that the crystals are arranged at right angles to the surface, while those of the inner layer are lamellate, a term meaning that they are arranged parallel to the surface. In some shells the middle layer may be

more complex and consist of several regions. The innermost layer, depending on the mineral content, may be porcellaneous or nacreous; a nacreous layer consists of the beautiful iridescent material we know as mother-of-pearl.

Some shells have a much thicker inner layer than others and if this layer is nacreous, this is the area where pearls are produced. If a particle of sand or some other foreign body gets trapped between the tissues of the animal this stimulates the gland cells of the mantle to secrete nacre around it. Layer upon layer may be laid down in an attempt to neutralize the irritation, and eventually a pearl is built up around the offending substance. If the inner layer is porcellaneous, the presence of a foreign body has the same effect but the 'pearl' formed has a dull lustre, like marble.

The periostracum may be ridged, forming spines or hairs, but in some molluscs it is nearly transparent. It usually wears away easily, so it is often partially or wholly absent from the surface of shells that are washed ashore by the tide. Many shell collectors deliberately remove the periostracum to expose the colour patterns of the shell beneath. Certain molluscs have no periostracum at all; in these the surface of the shell is glossy and during the animal's life the mantle extends out and over the shell.

Ridges or lines running parallel to the edge are visible on most shells, and these indicate periods when the gland cells of the mantle are inactive. If the length of time between two such rest periods is known, then the age of the shell can be calculated. Unfortunately this is only known for some molluscs, so often it is not possible to judge a shell's age. Size is not necessarily an indication of age either, because in two molluscs of the same species and age, the one that inhabits an area with a prolific food supply will grow much faster than the one that lives in an area with a poor food supply. Temperature variations and water salinity also affect the rate of growth. Most molluscs continue to grow throughout their lives, although at a diminishing rate, but some cease to grow after reaching sexual maturity and any shell formed after this simply increases the thickness.

The minerals and substances secreted by the gland cells to produce the shell are derived from the food the animal eats. So too, presumably, are the pigments which give the shell its attractive colours. These pigments become concentrated in colour-depositing cells in the mantle edge and their position determines the colour pattern produced on the shell. With growth the intensity and shade of colour may change because of variations in the salinity of the water or in the creature's diet. Unusual shell shapes, such as spines and knobs, are formed when the outer region of the mantle divides into small sections or branches as the shape of the shell follows the shape of the mantle edge.

Besides the presence of the shell the other characteristic features of the Mollusca are a large muscular foot for locomotion and special gills for breathing. These gills, called ctenidia, are feathery structures suspended within the mantle cavity, the space between the mantle and the body of the animal. While it is alive a constant flow of water is maintained through this cavity, which aerates the gills.

The variety of form within this phylum ranges from a small sea snail to a large ten-armed squid. Scientists therefore, have divided this vast group into five classes, two of which contain the majority of all seashells. These are the Gastropoda and the

5

Lamellibranchia. They themselves are such large classes that it is necessary to divide them into smaller and smaller groups with similar characteristics until the individual type or species is reached. A word about this classification system, which we shall be using throughout this book. It seems complicated, but is really quite straightforward and extremely informative. Because common names differ throughout the world zoologists always use Latin names. For instance, the arthritic spider conch is *Lambis arthritica* and the orange spider conch *Lambis crocata*. We can tell that the two species are closely related, because they both have the same first or genus name — the second name being that of the species. The queen conch is *Strombus gigas* and the hawk-wing conch *Strombus raninus*; obviously, these two species also belong to one genus, but a different one. Both the true conches and the spider conches have a flaring outer lip, although its form is slightly different. From this we can deduce that the two genera are closely related, and indeed they are included in one group or family, called the Strombidae. A grouping of similar families is called a superfamily, a group of superfamilies is called an order and a group of orders makes up the class, which in this example is the Gastropoda. Beyond that is the primary division, the phylum. The diagram shows the relationship, up to the stage of the family.

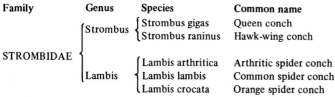

Family	Genus	Species	Common name
	Strombus	Strombus gigas	Queen conch
		Strombus raninus	Hawk-wing conch
STROMBIDAE			
	Lambis	Lambis arthritica	Arthritic spider conch
		Lambis lambis	Common spider conch
		Lambis crocata	Orange spider conch

Some families have representatives in all the world's oceans, as, for example, the family Mytilidae, the mussels; others are confined to one area like the family Tridacnida, the giant clams, which are restricted to the coral reefs of the Indo-Pacific oceans.

The Gastropoda or univalves, as they are commonly called, have a single shell which is usually coiled. Its apex is the region that was first formed when the animal was in its larval stage. As it grows the shell is laid down in a series of whorls, and the last and largest of these, the one that contains the aperture, is called the body whorl. The aperture may be entire or it may have an indentation, which is called the siphonal groove. Every gastropod has a large foot with a flat sole to equip it for crawling over surfaces, and in some species this foot bears a horny disc or plug, called the operculum, which fits neatly into the aperture to close the shell after the animal has retracted its body. Above the foot is a distinct head, which bears tentacles, eyes and mouth, and the body, which is asymmetrical, twists to enable it to be completely withdrawn into the shell. This is the form we know so well in snails, and many marine species of snail produce beautiful seashells. However, slugs are also included in the Gastropoda, and it is worth recalling that they have a reduced shell or no shell at all and a body that is straight and symmetrical.

The Lamellibranchia (Pelecypoda) or bivalves have the shell formed of two valves which are hinged together by an elastic ligament and held closed by strong muscles. The body is laterally flattened so that it fits between the two valves, but there is no distinct head, just a mouth, and the foot is flattened so that it can be protruded between the valves for burrowing. Most bivalves are comparatively inactive animals living below the surface of the sand or mud, but a few have special modifications for living on the surface. This class, like the Gastropoda, has many marine species that produce attractive seashells.

The Scaphopoda or tusk shells have a tubular shell which is open at both ends, but wider at one end than the other and slightly curved, thus giving it a tusklike shape. The foot is trilobed and when the animal is burrowing, it protrudes through the wider end of the shell while the narrow end projects above the surface of the sand in order to take in water. All scaphopods live offshore and are seashells of interest to the collector, although the number of known species is limited.

The Amphineura (Placophora) or chitons have an elongated shell formed of eight articulating plates so that when disturbed the animal can curl up and thus protect the body tissues. A chiton can cling to rock surfaces with its large foot, but not so closely as the gastropod limpets. Chitons are not included here under seashells.

The Cephalopoda include the cuttlefish, squids and octopuses; these have reduced internal skeletons and are the most highly developed molluscs. They cannot, however, be described as seashells, but this class does include the pearly or chambered nautili, whose spectacular external shell is always a favourite with seashell enthusiasts. There are many fossil forms of this group, but only a few living species are known today and they are confined to warm waters. The shell is chambered, and the body of the animal is always contained in the outermost chamber.

Molluscs are found inhabiting all the habitats of the sea and shore from the highest area reached by the tide to the depths of the oceans. They are most abundant in the region that extends between the highest point on the shore splashed by the sea and the edge of the continental shelf. Each species of mollusc is uniquely adapted to its own particular niche in the marine communities.

Rocky coasts support large and varied molluscan populations because they can find ample protection amongst the cracks and crevices and under the thick carpets of seaweeds when the tide recedes and the animals are exposed to the atmosphere. Another advantage is that many other marine creatures also live among the rocks, thus ensuring an ample food supply for the molluscs that are carnivorous. Many of the shore species become inactive when they are exposed at low tide but as soon as the tide

Right
This limpet has been removed from its rock to show the basic structure of a mollusc. On the right the shell is just visible outside the edge of the mantle, and the mantle cavity is the space extending between the mantle and the large foot; the head with its tentacles protrudes behind. Notice the pieces of broken stone attached to the foot, they indicate how tenaciously this species adheres to the rock surface.

Left
This china clam shows the typical structure of a bivalve. In life the two valves were hinged together and the orange line is the remains of the elastic ligament that joined them. The attractive curly edge of the two halves are matched so that when the shell closes they fit tightly together.

returns they start moving around in search of food. Fortunately, even when the tide is out the movements and activities of these animals can still be watched in rock pools — and this is a fascinating pastime.

Ecological studies of the living molluscs show that there the various species are found in zones, depending upon the period of exposure to the atmosphere on the shore and to the depth of water in the shallow seas. The majority of molluscs in rocky areas regularly move about searching for food, so most of them are univalves. Some of them feed on the seaweeds, and consequently are herbivorous; others feed on marine creatures and so are carnivorous, while the scavengers, which feed on dead and decaying organic matter, are omnivorous. Some of the non-burrowing species of bivalve, such as the mussels, which attach themselves to surfaces by tough threads, live on the rocks, and a few bivalves actually live *within* the rocks. These latter, such as the piddocks, bore into the rock and remain inside it throughout their lives, feeding on plankton that is drawn in along with the seawater.

Sandy coasts and shallow seas support vast populations of burrowing molluscs, but the variety of species is not so great as on rocky coasts. The bivalves are admirably adapted for this mode of life with their flattened foot for digging down into the sand and their method of feeding by filtering food particles from the indrawn water. Here, too, are found some univalves which shuffle along in the surface sand in search of prey.

Muddy shores are also inhabited by large populations of burrowing forms, but the number of different species is even smaller than on sandy shores. This is probably because muddy areas occur around estuaries, so that the animals have to contend with varying salinity as well as the very fine mud particles, and only a few species are properly adapted for these conditions. In the tropics, mangrove swamps harbour both univalves and bivalves, although many of them are attached to the mangrove roots or move over their surface rather than burrowing in the mud.

Many of the most colourful and artistic seashells are those of the molluscs that live in or on coral reefs. These reefs, found only in warm waters, are formed from coral, the limy exo-skeletons of sedentary coelenterate animals which live in large colonies; only the upper coral contains the live animals, which are minute polyps similar to sea anemones. Coral reefs are full of crevices, and these give the molluscs the same sort of protection as a rocky shore. Some bivalves actually become embedded in the coral, and grow at approximately the same rate as it does to prevent themselves from being smothered.

Other organisms often live on the surface of molluscan shells forming an encrusting growth, so that in their natural habitat they are almost unrecognizable as the colourful seashells known to the collector.

Marine molluscs are found in all the world's seas, but the warm tropical waters support those with the larger, more colourful and elaborate shells; the seashells from cooler waters look quite drab in comparison. Also there is a far greater variety of species in tropical seas than in cooler ones. The richest of all molluscan communities are found in the Indo-Pacific. This large region extends from the coast of East Africa eastwards across the Indian Ocean, through the East Indies, to the Pacific islands, and also extends southward to the coast of northern Australia and northward to take in part of the coast of China.

When the rough sea calms down after a
storm many shallow water animals are
stranded high on the shore, including both
univalves and bivalves. This is a good time
to go shell collecting. Here are some of
the shells deposited on a North Atlantic
shore. The razor shell on the left shows
the foot at the bottom, the body tissue
between the valves and the siphon at the
top. Other shells include venus, carpet,
pelican's foot, turret, otter shell, whelk
and periwinkle. In the right-hand bottom
corner can be seen the carapace of an
edible crab and the arms of a burrowing
starfish.

Left
The brown markings on this spindle shell
are the remains of the periostracum, the
protective outer layer of the shell. In the
live specimen this would probably have
been intact, but much of it has been worn
away by friction as the empty shell was
rolled shorewards by the tide. The
photograph also clearly shows the
structure of a gastropod shell with a
siphonal groove, and the dull colour
indicates that it is found in cool waters.
This species, *Colus gracilus*, approximately
7 cm long, inhabits the eastern area of the
North Atlantic, but other similar species
live off the coast of North America.

Above
The majority of bivalves live buried in the
sand or mud, but the various species of

mussel live on the surface attached to
rocks. They have the basic structure of all
bivalves, but they secrete a sticky
substance which hardens into tough
threads that anchor them to the
substratum. When exposed at low water
the two valves are tightly clamped
together, but when the tide returns the
valves open slightly and the edge of the
mantle becomes visible, as shown here.
Water is then drawn in through the
opening bounded by the frilled edge of
the mantle and expelled through the
opening with the straight edge; mussels
feed by filtering plankton from the
indrawn water. This cool-water species,
which inhabits the rocky coasts of
Europe and North America, is the
edible mussel, *Mytilus edulis*, which may
reach a length of 7.5 cm.

Right
In comparison with something like the
orange spider conch this is a dull shell and
therefore is an inhabitant of cooler waters.
This bivalve lives in sand or muddy gravel
below the mean tide level around the
southern and western coasts of the British
Isles and along the Atlantic coast of
Europe. The shell is sculptured with
radiating ribs and concentric grooves
giving it a cross-cut pattern. This
particular cross-cut carpet shell,
Venerupis decussata, measured 4.5 cm
in length but a large specimen may
reach 7 cm.

Right

Here is an example of a bivalve with a
thick, ridged periostracum extended into
spines. In life small shell fragments and
particles of sand become trapped on this
uneven surface; maybe this helps to
camouflage the mollusc and thus protect
it from predators. This is the bearded
horse mussel, *Modiolus barbatus*, which,
like all mussels, lives attached to the
surface of rocks by tough threads. It
inhabits the lower shore and shallow
waters along the North Atlantic coasts
from Great Britain to Morocco and
extends into the Mediterranean. A large
specimen may be 6 cm long.

Far right

Scallops are another group of bivalves
which do not burrow, but live on the
surface; however, they are not attached
to the rocks like the mussels. They live on
the bottom of the sea, and are capable of
swimming short distances by rapidly
flapping their shell valves. They rise
from the bottom, zigzag through the
water a little way and then drop back to
the sea floor. The edge of the mantle of
scallops is extended into sensory
tentacles, and in this beautiful scallop
from the coral reefs of Mozambique,
Africa, these are seen protruding
between the two valves.

Right

These red nose cockles have been stranded
ashore after a storm. Because the animals
are dead the muscles which normally hold
the two valves together are no longer
functional, and so the tissues of the body
are exposed. The 'red nose' is the large,
elongated, bright red foot used in
burrowing. In the specimen on the left
the mantle can be seen, although it is
partially torn away from the upper shell.
There are several different species of
large, solid-shelled cockles which are
included under the heading 'red nose'.
This is the spiny cockle, *Cardium
echinatum*, which burrows in sand
below the low-water mark around
European coasts and can be 7.6 cm long.

Right
The argonauts or paper nautili are
cephalopods similar to the octopuses
except that the female secretes a special
receptacle for carrying the eggs until they
hatch, and this is the fragile but
handsome 'shell'. No such structure is
produced by the much smaller male,
hence it is not a true shell like that of
other molluscs. This 'shell', *Argonauta
nodosa*, may be 25 cm long and is found
in all warm seas.

Below
Cowrie shells do not have a periostracum;
the surface of the shell is smooth and
glossy, as shown here in the ocellate
cowrie, *Cypraea ocellata.* In a live cowrie
the mantle lobes are very large and
extend outside the shell, almost
completely covering it. This species is
beautifully patterned with black dots in
the centre of white circles that look like
small eyes on a buff background. This is a
small species with a maximum length of

2.5 cm, which is confined to the warm
waters of the Indian Ocean and was
uncommon until with more extensive
exploration covering wide areas it was
frequently found.

Right
The pearly or chambered nautili are the
only cephalopods with an external coiled
shell. The shell is single but differs from
that of univalves because its interior is
divided into chambers. In the living
animal, these contain air or gas to give it
buoyancy and the animal controls the
quantity as required for floating,
swimming or moving over the sea floor.
The animal lives in the youngest outer
section, and can withdraw completely
into the large aperture. The chambered
section of this species, *Nautilus pompilus*,
is marked with reddish-brown wavy bands
and near the aperture with a black area;
beneath the outer layer the shell is pearly.
As the animal grows it moves forward,
sealing off the chamber just occupied by
a nacreous partition so that its body
always occupies the outermost chamber;
however, a small hole is always left in
each partition so that all the chambers
are connected. This species may reach a
diameter of 15-20 cm. It inhabits the
tropical waters of the Indo-Pacific,
particularly in the region of the
Philippine Islands.

Right
Mother-of-pearl is the nacreous layer of a
shell and its beautiful lustre can be seen
on the inner surfaces of this saddle oyster.
This is another bivalve which does not
burrow; it lives on the surface attached
firmly to rocks, the shells of other
molluscs, or any hard surface below
low-water mark. It secretes byssus
threads like the mussel, which pass from
the inner surface of the upper valve,
down through the hole in the lower valve,
onto the rock below; they are so
impregnated with brine that the mussel
seems to be cemented in position. The
shell is held so closely to its base in fact,
that as it grows the lower valve follows
the shape of the rock surface. Saddle
oysters or jingle shells are easy to
recognize by the hole in the lower valve,
but it is more difficult to identify the
different species. This is *Anomia
ephippium*, an eastern Atlantic species
which ranges from Iceland to South
Africa, and can be 6 cm long.

Left
In some gastropods the foot is very large,
with lateral extensions capable of folding
back to cover part or all of the shell when
the animal is moving over the substratum.
This is the girdled ancilla, *Ancillista
velesiana*, crawling along over the sand
on its voluminous foot. The shell surface
is shiny, which indicates that the ancillas
are another family that does not have a
periostracum. The girdled ancilla may
grow to a length of 6.5 cm and it inhabits
deep water where the bottom is sandy
along the coast of New South Wales,
Australia.

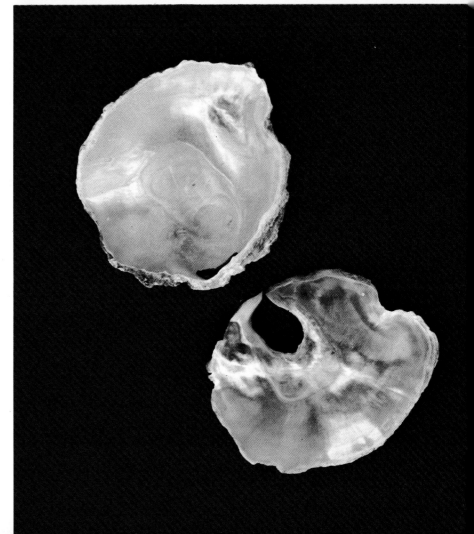

These photographs both show the internal structure of univalves, with the central axis, the columella, extending from apex to base. The cavities of the whorls indicate how the body of the animal has to twist in order to fit into the confined space. *Right* is a turret shell in which the numerous whorls increase uniformly in size, whereas in the turban shell *far right* there are only four whorls, which rapidly increase in size to the large body whorl. In the turban shell the sutures are deep and clearly marked and each whorl is distinctly bulbous, but in the turret shell the sutures are simple lines and the outer surface of the shell is straight and hardly indicates the position of the whorls within. In the cut edge of the turban shell the outer porcellaneous and inner nacreous layers can be clearly seen and the pearly nature of the inner surface of the whorls is obvious.

Univalves or single shells

All univalve molluscs have a single shell with the same basic spiral form of a central column, the columella, around which the shell is laid down in whorls. The pointed tip, called the apex, is the first region to be secreted in the larval stage and as the animal grows the whorls it produces gradually increase in size in order to accommodate the developing body. The youngest and largest whorl is called the body whorl and this has the opening to the exterior, known as the aperture. In some families the edge of the aperture is always smooth and continuous — zoologists call it entire — but in others the edge is deeply grooved and sometimes extended into a canal-like structure, and then it is said to be siphonate. The other whorls continuing up to the apex constitute the spire of the shell. The spire may be sharply pointed, elongated, short or flattened. Seen from the outside, the junction between neighbouring whorls is marked by a line, called a suture, which may be fine and smooth or partially indented, and sometimes the whorls flare out into a shoulder which may be thickened and bear knobs or spines.

When a univalve shell is cross-sectioned from the apex to the base the cavities of the whorls can be seen within spiralling around the columella, and in life the body of the animal is adapted to twist around this central axis and fit comfortably into the available space. In the mature animal, however, the body often does not extend into the smaller, older whorls near the apex. A special muscle attaches the body to the columella and it is the contraction and relaxation of this columellar muscle which controls the animal's withdrawal into and extrusion from the shell. Of course, only the head and foot are ever protruded outside the shell, as in the case of the common garden snail.

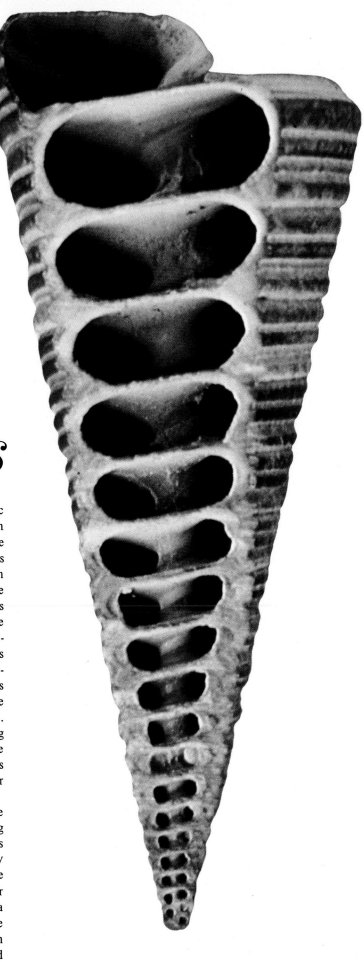

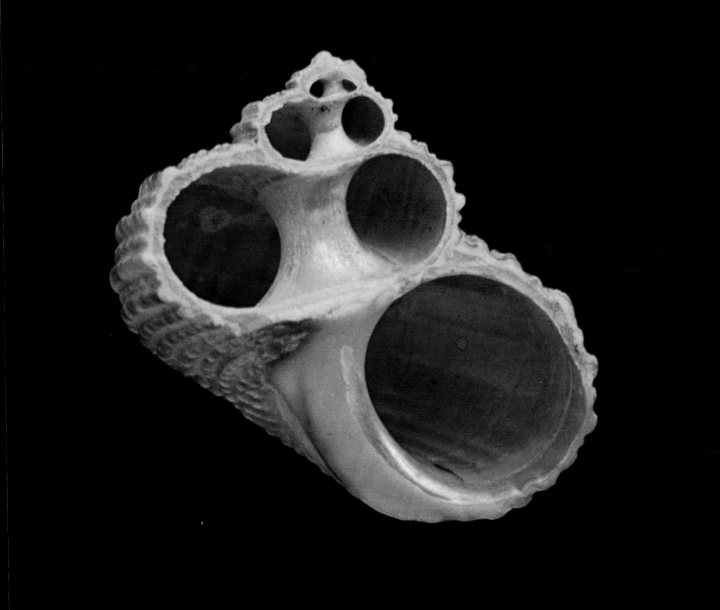

When the body is retracted the aperture may be closed by an operculum; this is either a limy plug or a disc-like horny structure with growth lines comparable to those on the shell. The edge of the aperture next to the columella is referred to as the inner lip and the free edge as the outer lip and in some species these lips bear ridges or "teeth".

When a univalve shell is observed from above — that is, looking down on the apex — the whorls are seen to run in a spiral. This usually runs in a clockwise direction, and such a shell is said to be dextral. Also when a dextral shell is held upright (apex uppermost) the aperture is situated on the right. However, in a few species the direction of the spiral is anticlockwise, and these are referred to as sinistral shells. Occasionally a shell coils in the opposite direction to the one that is normal for the species and such a shell is considered a collector's piece. The size of a univalve shell is measured by its length from the tip of the apex to the lowest part of the body whorl.

All univalves are active molluscs moving around on their large, flat muscular foot in search of food, but some are herbivorous and others carnivorous. Nevertheless all have a specialized tonguelike structure in the mouth called a radula. This is a chitinous or horny ribbon which bears teeth; the herbivores have many small teeth for rasping vegetation from the rocks, but in carnivores the teeth are larger and fewer in number for cutting through the flesh of the prey.

Univalves — Aperture Entire

Univalves with an entire or continuous aperture usually have a wide body whorl and in some species only the body whorl remains in the adult stage. The majority are herbivores and therefore live in fairly shallow waters where the vegetation is abundant.

Abalones (Family: Haliotidae) have a tiny spire and a very large flattened body whorl with an enormous aperture, one edge of which turns inwards. A row of holes runs parallel with this incurved edge, a feature which makes abalone shells easy to identify. In the living abalone sea water passes under the edge of the shell into the mantle cavity to aerate the gills, and is afterwards expelled through these holes. The inner surface of the shell is nacreous.

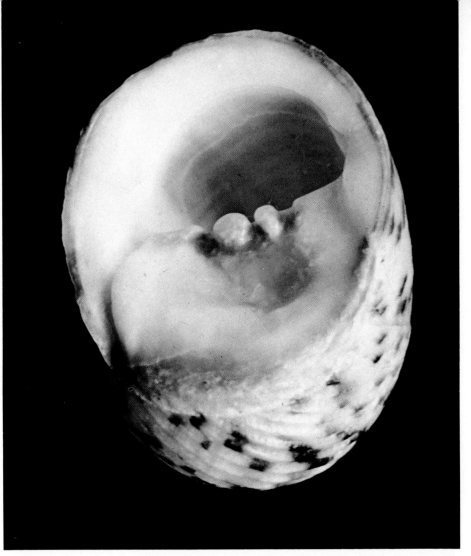

Right
Two pronounced teeth are present on the inner lip of this nerite shell and the orange-red blotch on the flattened area behind identifies it as the bleeding-tooth shell, *Nerita peloronta.* The spire is low and the body whorl enlarged so that the shell is somewhat oval; it can grow to a length of 2.5 cm. Like all nerites it is a vegetarian and is a common inhabitant of the intertidal rocks along the coast of southeastern Florida; its range extends southwards to the West Indies.

Far right
This unique shell with spines radiating from the periphery of the body whorl is the triumphant star, *Guildfordia triumphans.* It has a flat base, low spire and the cavities of the individual whorls are narrow. The inner surface is nacreous and nacre can also be seen on some of the older spines where the outer surface has been worn away. The spines are hollow and may number seven to nine in this species. As growth occurs and new shell and spines are formed the old spines are dissolved by the animal and only a tiny trace of the lost spines is left at the sutures, as seen here. The triumphant star is a vegetarian which lives in deep water off the coast of Japan. The diameter across the body whorl of this particular specimen is 3.5 cm and the height 2 cm, but these shells often grow to more than twice this size.

Keyhole Limpets (Family: Fissurelidae) have only a conical body whorl with a perforation in the top which is analogous to the holes in abalone shells.

True Limpets (Family: Patellidae) have no spire, just a conical body whorl.

None of the molluscs in these three families can withdraw the body completely into the shell; instead they cling closely to the substratum for protection by means of the strong muscular foot. The hold of the limpets is particularly strong and suction-like, hence the expression 'to cling like a limpet'.

Top Shells (Family: Trochidae) are univalves with the normal shell structure of a spire and a large body whorl, but are typically pyramidal in shape. The nacreous layer is thick and the operculum thin, horny and round to fit into the aperture.

Turban Shells (Family: Turbinidae) are similar to top shells but are slightly more elongated and rounded so that the shape does indeed resemble a turban. The operculum is different also, being hard and limy, and in some species it is so highly polished that it is called a "cat's eye". Some are so attractive that they are used in the manufacture of shell jewellery such as bracelets and earrings.

Nerite Shells (Family: Neritidae) are solid with a somewhat flattened spire, large body whorl and a smooth, flat area next to the inner lip, which is strongly toothed.

Periwinkles (Family: Littorinidae) have a small, solid shell with only a few whorls and are one of the commonest univalves found in the intertidal zone of rocky shores the world over.

Turret Shells (Family: Turritellidae) are easily identified by the long spire consisting of many whorls and terminating in a sharp point at the apex. The whorls gradually increase in size, giving the shell a symmetrical tapered form.

Sundials or Staircase Shells (Family: Architectonicidae) are solid, regularly coiled shells with narrow whorls which gradually and uniformly increase in size. Viewed from above, the apex appears to be in the centre of the circular base. The umbilicus is large and open to the apex and as the inner margin of each whorl is notched when viewed from below it looks like a spiral staircase. Sundials are attractively patterned shells.

Violet Snail Shells (Family: Janthinidae) are very fragile usually globular in shape with few whorls, but a large body whorl. They are a delicate mauve or purple and are unique molluscs because they are pelagic and drift in the surface waters. They form a float by trapping air bubbles in mucus which is secreted by and attached to the foot. Should the snail become detached from this float it sinks to the bottom and dies because it is unable to regain the surface. These violet snails are carnivorous and feed on the animal components of the plankton.

Slipper Limpets (Family: Calyptraeidae) do not belong to the same family as the true limpets although they grip the surface in a similar way with the muscular foot. The slipper limpet shell, which has a reduced spire, has a large oval body whorl with a shelf or ledge extending halfway across the aperture to support the soft parts of the animal. These molluscs are sedentary and are often found in chains of up to 12. An interesting feature is that the oldest specimens at the bottom of the chain are females and the youngest at the top are males, with a few inbetween which are hermaphrodite. Another unusual feature is that they are filter feeders like the bivalves.

Above

True limpets inhabit the rocky shores of temperate seas throughout the world. They cling to the rock surface tenaciously with the large flat foot and draw the shell down tightly to survive the buffeting of gale force waves. In fact, they are one of the few animals which can live on the most exposed rocky shores. Limpets are conical univalves formed of the body whorl only, but the shape may vary somewhat within a species, depending on the environment. For example, limpets that inhabit exposed rocks have a sharply conical shell whereas those in sheltered positions have a more flattened cone. When submerged they move around but before the tide ebbs they return to their original position. Limpets living on soft rock eventually form a groove where they continually clamp down on the same spot, and these are called 'homing rings'. Most limpets have a fairly smooth edge to the shell, but in this South African species it is uneven; this is the spiked limpet, *Patella longicosta*, which can be some 7.5 cm in diameter.

Left
There is no spire in the keyhole limpet,
only the body whorl with a hole in the
apex. The development of this hole is
interesting — in the minute young only a
slit is present in the edge of the shell, but
as growth occurs this gradually closes
over to form a hole which, with further
secretion of shell, eventually becomes
situated towards the centre in the adult.
These molluscs are vegetarians that live
in the shallow waters of rocky coasts and
there are several hundred different
species.

This page
It is easy to see why this delightful shell
is known as the strawberry top. These
pretty markings are typical of *Clanculus
pharonium*, which inhabits the shallow
tropical waters of the Indian Ocean. It is
a small shell, growing only to a height of
about 2.4 cm, with a deep umbilicus. The
inner lip is strongly toothed and the outer
lip uneven with black dots along its
margin. In the upright picture *above* the
aperture appears on the right; this
indicates that it is a dextral shell.

Far left
This turban shell can be distinguished from a top shell by its more elongated and rounded shape and greater indentation of the sutures. Turbans are strong shells and the animal has a hard operculum attached to the foot which fits extremely tightly into the aperture when the body is completely retracted. This gives excellent protection against predators. This gold-mouthed turban, *Turbo chrysostomus*, is identified by the yellow or golden aperture which contrasts with the white lips. It can be 7 cm long. Coral reefs are its habitat, and it is particularly common on the Great Barrier Reef.

Left
The lovely violet snail mollusc always floats this way up, with its aperture towards the ocean surface, because its raft of air bubbles is attached to the foot. When washed ashore *en masse* these molluscs form a delicate mauve carpet along the edge of the sea. Because the shells are so fragile, unfortunately many become broken. Violet snails are carnivorous, feeding on small jellyfish and other tiny creatures of the plankton, as well as on the purple sail jellyfish or by-the-wind sailor, *Velella velella*, which is considerably larger than the snails themselves. Different species of this snail are found in the warm seas of the world. This is the common violet snail, *Janthina janthina*, which is about 2.5 cm high and floats in the warm surface waters of the Atlantic.

Left
Dextral or right-handed coiling is clearly shown in this attractive top shell. Start at the apex and follow the whorls round — the direction is clockwise. This is the giant button top shell, *Umbonium giganteum*, which inhabits muddy bays in Japan. The spire is greatly flattened; this gives the shell a squat appearance because the diameter is approximately twice the height. The diameter of this specimen is 3.0 cm. As with many top shells, part of the outer surface has been worn away and the nacreous layer below is exposed.

Right
This West Indian top shell, *Cittarium pica*, has a large, well-defined, deep umbilicus and the entire aperture is clearly seen. It is a heavy shell and has a thick nacreous layer; the pearly surface can be seen within the aperture. The body whorl is wide and the living animal completely withdraws its body into the shell, closing the aperture with a circular, horny operculum. The shell has the typical pyramidal shape of all top shells, but the number of whorls is small. The length and diameter are approximately equal and may reach 8 cm. This species is abundant around rocks lying low on the shore in the West Indies; consequently, the animal is sometimes eaten as a component of fish chowders.

Previous pages
The shadow emphasizes the conical shape
of these European limpets. The rock
around the animals is bare of vegetation;
this is because the limpets browse on any
seaweed sporelings which encrust the
surface, thus preventing colonization by
the mature plants. When covered by the
sea these limpets move around in search
of vegetation. This is the common limpet,
Patella vulgata, which may grow to a
diameter of 5.5 cm.

Right
The beautiful patterning and colouring of
the Atlantic sundial, *Architectonica
nobilis*, is so impressive that once seen it
is not likely to be forgotten. The
clockwise coiling is uniform with a very
gradual increase in the width of the
individual whorls. It is a low, squat shell
with a diameter that is nearly twice its
height. The diameter of this specimen is
5.8 cm and the height 3 cm. *Far right*
shows the large, deep umbilicus with the
spiral staircase form; notice the ridges on
the inner margin of the whorls. Sundial
shells are also distinguished by the
narrowness of the aperture and cavity of
each whorl; this indicates that the body
of the animal inside must be somewhat
elongated. There are some 40 different
species of sundial shells and all live in
tropical waters. This Atlantic sundial lives
in sandy areas of the Atlantic from the
southeastern coast of North America to
the West Indies.

Left
This slipper limpet can be recognized by
its oval shape and the shelf partway across
the aperture. For a univalve it has a most
unusual mode of feeding; it is a filter
feeder, a method normally associated
with bivalves. Most univalves actively
search for food, but the slipper limpet is
a sedentary creature and so depends on
food being carried to it by the water
currents. Because of this, slipper limpets
are considered pests on oyster beds
because they compete with the oysters
for planktonic food; they also tend to
smother the oysters. This is *Crepidula
fornicata*, a common American species
some 5 cm long, which was unfortunately
introduced into European waters along
with the American oysters which were
brought to England to replenish the
oyster beds of the east coast towards the
end of the nineteenth century.

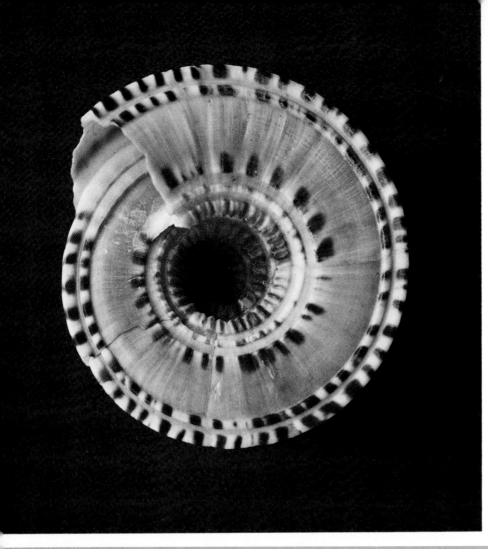

Below
Top shells of the genus *Calliostoma* are
finely sculptured, often with delicately
coloured markings, and grow to a height
of some 2.5 cm. This is the common or
painted top shell, *Calliostoma
zizyphinum*, which has a flat base and
regular pyramidal form. The red streaks
on the yellowish-pink ground colour are
typical of the species but the green is due
to encrusting algae. In the specimen on
the right the horny operculum with its
concentric growth lines can be clearly
seen. Like all top shells this species is
vegetarian. It lives low on the shore and
in shallow water along the rocky coasts
of Europe. Other species of the same
genus inhabit similar waters all over the
world.

Right
This solid spindle-shaped shell with the
long body whorl and ridged inner lip
edging the elliptical aperture is typical
of mitre shells, which inhabit warm
shallow waters and feed on worms
and bivalves. This is the papal mitre,
Mitra papalis, which is one of the
handsomest mitres found in the
Indo-Pacific and may be 10 cm long.

Siphonate univalves

Many gastropods have a tubular structure, the siphon, which can
be extended outside the shell. This is formed by the folding of
the mantle edge and its function is to ensure that clear water is
drawn into the mantle cavity even when the animal is moving
through sand or mud, because sand particles would clog the
gills. To make it easier for the animal to protrude this siphon
the edge of the aperture of the shell is indented to form a
siphonal groove. In some species this groove is elongated into a
definite canal which may be open, partially closed or completely
closed over.

Univalves with a siphonate aperture have a more elongated
shape than those with an entire aperture: the body whorl is
longer than it is broad and the aperture is correspondingly oval
or even reduced to a slit. Most are carnivorous and some can
bore holes in other molluscan shells and suck out the juicy flesh
through them, while a few species secrete a poisonous fluid
which paralyzes the prey.

Conches or Strombs (Family: Strombidae) are sometimes
referred to as wing shells because of the flaring, thickened outer
lip, which typically bears a U-shaped notch towards the siphonal
groove. The probable function of this notch is to enable the
right eye to be protruded, because its eye stalk is shorter than
that of the left eye. The foot is long and narrow, with a
sickle-shaped operculum which the animal uses as a lever in
moving over the surface in a series of leaps and for righting itself
when overturned. The shell is solid and young specimens are
difficult to identify because they do not have the extended
outer lip and therefore look like cone shells. The periostracum is
thin and bears considerable algal growths which give excellent
camouflage as the stromb moves along in search of its food of

algae or detritus. The inner layer of the shell is porcellaneous and beautiful pink pearls may be formed in the large queen conch of the West Indies. All these species live in tropical waters.

Also included in this family are the spider conches, which have acquired this common name from the slender, elongated spines of the outer lip. All the nine species, which can be identified by the number and shape of the spines, live in the shallow tropical waters of the Indo-Pacific.

Pelican's Foot Shells (Family: Aporrhaidae) are closely related to the conches but the margin of the flaring outer lip extends into points so that it resembles a webbed foot.

Cowries (Family: Cypraeidae) are probably one of the best known univalves. They are easily recognized by the smooth, glossy surface of the elongated oval shell which has a long narrow aperture, bearing teeth on one or both lips, and with a posterior groove as well as the anterior siphonal groove. The spire is not apparent in a mature shell because the body whorl grows over it. Young specimens are difficult to identify as they have a thin shell with a spire and wide aperture thus somewhat resembling olive shells. However, when they near sexual maturity the body whorl becomes so swollen that it covers the spire and the outer lip turns inwards, narrowing the aperture to a mere slit. When the gonads are fully developed no further growth in size occurs, but instead the shell becomes thickened and teeth develop on the lips. The final size of the shell depends on the size it had attained when sexual maturity was reached and this may vary considerably within one species depending on environmental conditions and particularly on food supply. There is no periostracum and the mantle can extend outside to cover most of the shell surface, but if there is the slightest indication of danger, it is rapidly withdrawn.

Helmet Shells (Family: Cassididae) are solid and thick with a large flat, platelike area extending from the inner lip. The outer lip is thick and toothed, the siphonal canal short and the body whorl large with a somewhat elongated aperture. Some of the larger species resemble the shape of the helmets worn by the ancient Romans, and because of the thickness of the shell they have been used since early times for carving cameos.

Triton Trumpet Shells (Family: Cymatiidae) are large, thick, well-sculptured and beautifully patterned, with a short siphonal canal; they include amongst their number some of the largest univalves of the world. Most are tropical species and they move about sluggishly in search of starfish, their main diet.

Murex Shells (Family: Muricidae) are amongst the most ornamental of the univalves, with conspicuous spines, knobs or complex branching arms over the whole surface. They inhabit the tropical and semitropical waters of the world, but the most bizarre and colourful are found in tropical waters. Some species have a very long siphonal canal. They are carnivorous, and most species secrete a mauve or purple fluid.

Rock Shells (Family: Thaididae) include drupes, dog whelks (dogwinkles) and oyster drills, which are smaller and less ornate univalves than the closely related murex shells. (All belong to the same superfamily and sometimes the thaids are classified as a subfamily of the Muricidae.) They live among rocks or corals mostly in the intertidal zone and are carnivorous, feeding mainly on barnacles and other molluscs. Some prey on bivalves, including oysters, by drilling a hole in the shell and sucking out the succulent juices; it is no wonder that these oyster drills are considered pests by oystermen.

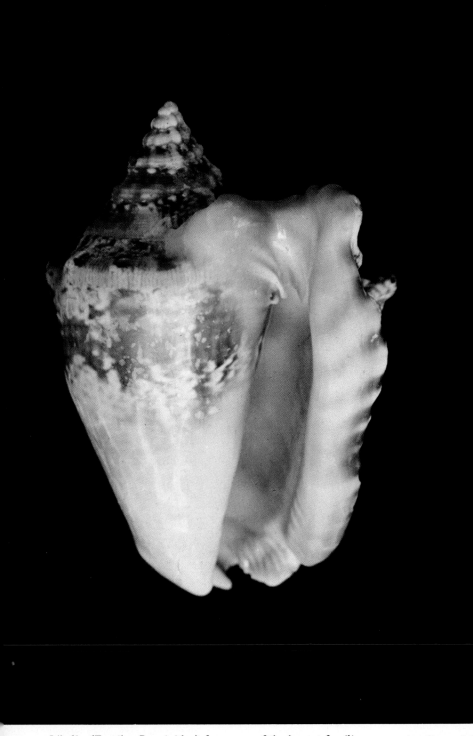

Whelks (Family: Buccinidae) form one of the largest families of marine univalves, with polar, temperate and tropical species. The shell is strong, the spire well-defined with indented sutures, the aperture fairly large and the distinct siphonal canal short or of moderate length. The cooler water species are large, but dull in colour with a thick periostracum. All are carnivorous; some feed on living prey only, but others are scavengers and can be caught in traps baited with dead fish.

Crown Conches and Giant Whelks (Family: Melongenidae) are closely related to whelks and belong to the same super-family. The family is small but includes the largest known species of gastropod, the Australian trumpet, *Syrinx aruanus*, which may reach a length of 70 cm. Crown conches are heavy shells with spines on the shoulders of the younger whorls, giving them a crownlike appearance.

Tulip and Spindle Shells (Family: Fasciolariidae) also belong to the same superfamily as the whelks, but they are more elongated and have longer spines and siphonal canals.

Ancilla and Olive Shells (Family: Olividae) are smooth and glossy with a fairly short spire, an elongated body whorl and aperture and no periostracum.

Chank Shells (Family: Xancidae) are large, heavy, pear-shaped shells with a short spire and strongly ridged inner lip.

Mitres (Family: Mitridae) are narrow, elongated shells with a pointed spire, well-defined teeth on the inner lip and a short siphonal canal. The periostracum is thin and transparent.

Volutes (Family: Volutidae) are large shells, often patterned and colourful, with a short spire, enlarged aperture and inner lip bearing distinct ridges. The family includes the large shells used as water carriers and balers.

Cones (Family: Conidae) are conical in shape, the spire being short and wide and the body whorl tapering smoothly to the siphonal canal, with a slitlike aperture. Unlike that of the volutes, the cone's inner lip is always smooth. This large family includes one of the rarest of collectors' shells, the Glory-of-the-sea, *Conus gloria-maris*.

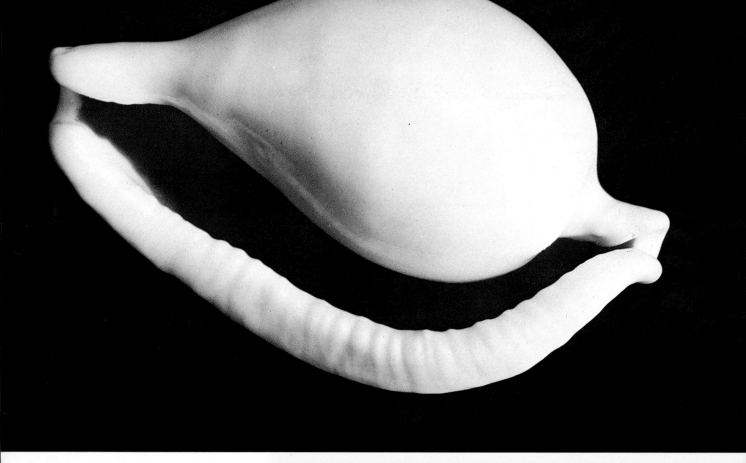

Right
The irregularly branched, longitudinal, clear pattern on the dorsal surface where the mantle edges meet gives the common name to this map cowrie, *Cypraea mappa.* Large specimens grow to a length of 8-10 cm and are usually found under coral slabs and stones in water between one and two metres deep in the Indian Ocean and most of the Pacific.

Centre
This X-ray photograph shows how the whorls of the cowrie overlap so that the exterior of the mature shell is smooth with no sign of the spire. The considerable thickening of the outer lip and formation of ridges or teeth can also be clearly seen, along with the typically elongated aperture.

Far right
This scorpion conch, *Lambis scorpius*, has six fingerlike processes plus the anterior siphonal canal. This shell is not completely mature because the siphonal canal is straight instead of curving at the tip to the right. A very young spider or scorpion conch has none of the spines that the mature mollusc has, but these gradually develop as the animal grows. The scorpion conch lives in shallow tropical waters of coral reef flats in the Indo-Pacific, and may be some 10-14 cm long.

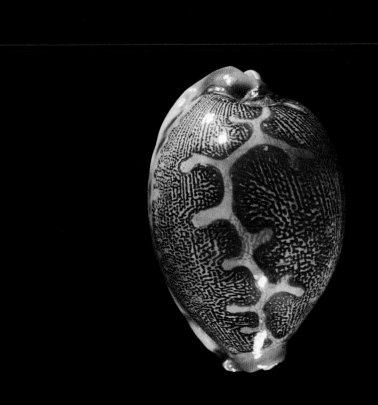

Left and right

The poached-egg cowrie, *Ovula ovum*, with its beautiful white shiny shell has, in contrast, a black body and black mantle spotted with white or yellow. The photograph *left* shows the typical elongated aperture of a cowrie shell and the attractive orange interior of this species. On the *right* the animal is crawling along on its large black foot with the mantle partly extended over the shell. The end of the siphon is just protruding and the white tips to the tentacles can be seen. The animal is feeding on its normal diet, large fleshy soft corals which abound where it lives in the warm waters of the Indo-Pacific. The poached-egg cowrie is one of the outstanding cowries of the Indo-Pacific; its shells are widely used by the natives as charms, ornaments, fertility symbols and in many other ways. Specimens may grow to 10-12 cm.

Right

It is easy to see why the name 'helmet shell' is used for this univalve. This is the king helmet, *Cassis tuberosa*, which lives in the shallow tropical waters of the Caribbean, moving over the sandy bottom in search of the sea urchins and sand dollars on which it feeds. This photograph clearly shows the solid nature of the shell with the large body whorl and flat, shiny triangular area bounding the inner lip. The aperture is narrow and the teeth are well defined on the outer lip. This species may grow to a length of some 17.5 cm.

Below

This true tulip shell, *Fasciolaria tulipa*, is common in shallow waters along the shores of Florida, but its range extends from North Carolina to the West Indies. The animal is sluggish and crawls along the sandy bottom in search of prey, often ploughing its way along with most of the shell buried, but with the siphon protruding above in order to draw in water. Specimens may reach a length of 13-15 cm.

Below right

The flattened spire, elongated body whorl with the long narrow aperture, and overall narrowing to the siphonal groove all identify this as a cone shell. This marble cone, *Conus marmoreus*, is a particularly handsome and distinctive species with its somewhat triangular white patches on a black background. It is a common inhabitant of coral reefs of the Indo-Pacific and grows to a length of 10 cm.

Above
This bull-mouth helmet, *Cypraecassis rufa*, is moving sluggishly over the surface with only the edge of the foot in view, but with the siphon extended for drawing in clear water. Notice how the two edges of the mantle meet to form this siphonal tube, and also note the eye which is exposed at the base of the nearest tentacle. This is an Indian Ocean species and can be 20 cm long.

Right
Drupe shells are small, solid shells with a knobbly surface, but the narrow aperture is bounded by wide, smooth, shiny lips bearing well-defined teeth. The aperture is usually of a bright contrasting colour and the majority are found on the intertidal reefs of the Indo-Pacific. This purple drupe, *Drupa morum*, with the violet aperture may grow to a length of 4 cm and is a common inhabitant of coral reefs throughout the Indo-Pacific.

Following pages
This *Murex denudatus* is so encrusted with other organisms that it is hard to believe that it has a number of spines on its surface. These are most probably for protection and also for camouflage, as can be seen from this photograph.

Right

It is easy to see by the sculpturing of this shell why it is called a crown conch. This beautiful species has well-indented sutures and attractive short spines on the shoulders of the younger whorls. This is the American crown conch, *Melongena corona*, which inhabits the intertidal areas of muddy shores of the southeastern United States from Florida to Mexico. It is a scavenger and can live in varying degrees of water salinity. The shell is heavy and can be 10 cm long.

Far right

This dilated whelk, *Penion dilatatus*, is a typical cold-water species of whelk, large, but drab in appearance, although sculptured attractively with deep grooves, sutures and slight bumps on the angular shoulders of the whorls. The oval aperture extends into a fairly long, open siphonal canal. This species inhabits New Zealand waters and may grow to a length of 17.5 cm.

Below right

The white siphon with its pink tip can just be seen protuding from the siphonal canal in this textile cone, *Conus textile*. The mottled foot extends from beneath the outer lip of the aperture. The true cone shape is obvious although the short spire is out of view. Like other cone shells this species is carnivorous and can paralyze its prey with a poisonous secretion. The radula, the tonguelike structure typical of univalves is specially modified with hollow teeth for the injection of this fluid, which is capable also of causing painful stings in humans. In fact, there have been a small number of human fatalities from cone stings. This textile cone, which can be 10 cm long, is common on the Great Barrier Reef and occurs throughout the Indo-Pacific.

Below

This X-ray photograph exhibits the typical form of whelk shells of the family Buccinidae. It shows the gradual but regular increase in the whorls' size around the columella and the large, though slightly elongated, aperture with a pronounced siphonal groove.

The raised teeth and deep grooves of the
hinge can clearly be seen on the inner
surface of the left valve of this warty
venus, *Venus verrucosa*, and the scar of
the anterior adductor muscle is just
visible. The shell is thick and the common
name is derived from the wartlike
tubercles on the concentric ridges; in
young specimens, however, these are not
so distinct and some difficulty in
identification may occur. The warty
venus is a suspension feeder and because
it is a shallow burrower the inhalent and
exhalent siphons are short. It lives in
sand or fine gravel from low on the shore
to a depth of 100 metres, and its range is
from the English Channel to South Africa;
it may grow to a length of 6 cm.

Bivalves

Bivalve molluscs have shells that consist of two halves or valves hinged together along the upper or dorsal edge by an elastic ligament. This ligament is easily broken when the empty shells are washed ashore so frequently only one valve of a pair is found along the driftline.

In the living creature the two valves can either be closed tightly together along the free edges or allowed to gape. The animal closes the valves by contracting a pair of strong adductor muscles, one of which connects the two valves anteriorly and the other posteriorly. When these muscles relax, the elastic thrust of the ligament forces the two valves apart.

The overall shape of bivalves varies. Some, like the giant clams, are symmetrical and in these the two adductor muscles are of equal size; others, such as the mussels and pen shells, are asymmetrical and here the anterior adductor muscle is much smaller. In the more rounded bivalves, like the scallops, the anterior adductor has completely disappeared and only the one large posterior muscle remains. It is this single muscle which forms the bulk of the edible portion of scallops. The points of attachment of these muscles can be seen as scars on the inner surface of the valves.

In some bivalves the hinge is strengthened by small ridges or teeth which fit into corresponding grooves in the opposite valve. The number, size, shape and position of these vary in different species and therefore are important aids in identifying the empty shells.

In the larval stage the shell is first formed near the centre of the hinge so that the youngest region is at the free margin, and concentric growth rings can be observed on many bivalve shells. In the majority of bivalves the two halves are similar but in a few they differ. For instance, in scallops the lower or right valve is convex, but the upper or left valve is flat.

In lamellibranch molluscs the mantle consists of two lobes, one on either side of the body, and each forms one valve of the shell. These mantle lobes are often joined along the free edges except for an opening for the foot and small apertures for the inflow and outflow of water to and from the mantle. Sometimes the mantle edge is drawn out into two siphons with the opening that inhales water at one tip and the opening that exhales it at the other. In species which are shallow burrowers, like the cockles, these siphons are short, but in deep burrowers such as otter shells they are quite long. The two siphons may be separate or fused together along most of their length. When extended, these siphons always protrude from the posterior of the shell and as their point of attachment leaves scars similar to those left by the mantle lobes on the inner surface of the valves, it is easy to identify the anterior and posterior in empty shells. The valves of deep burrowers are considerably flattened, which helps them to move through the sand or mud. The size of a bivalve shell is judged as being the length between the anterior and posterior margins.

Bivalve molluscs have an entirely different mode of life from that of univalves. They are sedentary animals; most of them remain buried throughout their lives, with only the tips of the siphons at the surface, simply waiting for food to come to them instead of going out to forage for it. They are filter feeders; this means they strain food particles from the indrawn water. The food may be the plankton of the sea or the detritus (minute pieces of dead organic matter) that lies on the ocean floor. In the plankton feeders the siphons are rigid and fairly broad, but in

Right
This beautiful pearl oyster, *Pinctada margaritifera*, is valuable in its own right as a source of mother-of-pearl, as well as occasionally producing perfect pearls. This species is known as the black lip because of the smoky-coloured band towards the shell margin and, along with the large golden lip, *Pinctada maxima*, is extensively fished off New Guinea and the northern and northwestern coasts of Australia. These two species give the finest quality of mother-of-pearl and usually the value of the shell fished exceeds that of the pearls sometimes found inside them. Although they are attached to stones by a byssus in the early stages, mature pearl oysters rest freely on the ocean floor. This black-lip pearl oyster is also fished in the Persian Gulf, but the largest specimens, up to 20 cm come from the tropical waters off northern Australia.

the detritus feeders they are long, narrow and flexible. The siphon that inhales water is longer than its companion so that it can circle a wide area of the sea floor in the search for suitable food particles.

The muscular foot is flattened to fit between the valves and its shape is well adapted for burrowing. In the cockles, which live just below the surface, the foot is also used to move the cockle over the surface of the sand. The foot is extended in a bent position but with the tip firmly touching the sand, then when the animal straightens the foot the shell rolls over.

A few bivalves live on the surface and are modified accordingly. The mussels live on rocks and stones and are held in position by means of tough threads extended around them like the guy ropes of a tent. The mussel secretes a sticky fluid which hardens on exposure to form the byssus, as these threads are called. The mussel twists around on its foot attaching the threads to the rocks in different directions, thus anchoring the shell so that it can be swayed slightly by the rippling of the tide, yet is held firmly enough not to be torn from its position. Others, such as saddle oysters and oysters, secrete a fluid which hardens into a cementlike byssus which holds the shell rigidly in place.

Some bivalves are specially adapted for boring into wood and rock. As larvae they deposit on the rock and start boring, gradually enlarging the burrow as they grow; this means that the opening is smaller than the end of the burrow so that the animal remains within it throughout its lifetime. The ship worm or teredo which does so much damage to wooden structures is not a true worm but a small bivalve mollusc.

Even more surprisingly, a few bivalves swim. The scallops

normally rest on the bottom, but they can move through the water by flapping their valves so that they appear to be taking "bites" at the water. They control their direction by the position through which they eject water from the mantle cavity. However, they can travel only a very short distance before dropping down to the sea floor again.

Bivalves include amongst their number the largest known molluscan shells; these are the giant clams of the tropical waters of the Indo-Pacific.

Pen Shells (Family: Pinnidae) are large, fragile, asymmetrical fan-shaped shells, which burrow with the narrow (anterior) end downwards.

Pearl Oysters (Family: Pteriidae) are rounded bivalves which rest on the bottom unattached. They have a thick nacreous layer and are valuable as a source of mother-of-pearl as well as of pearls; all inhabit tropical waters.

Hammer Oysters (Family: Isognomonidae) also natives of tropical waters, have an unusual hammer- or T-shape and are closely related to pearl oysters.

Mussels (Family: Mytilidae) are asymmetrical bivalves which live on the surface attached to rocks; they are ubiquitous but most abundant in temperate waters.

Saddle Oysters or Jingle Shells (Family: Anomiidae) are easily recognized by the large hole in the lower valve which allows byssus to pass through anchoring the shell to the rock below, and by the nacreous inner surface of both valves.

Scallops (Family: Pectinidae), which are found in all waters, have roundish shells with one large adductor muscle only and a reduced foot. The lower valve is convex, the upper flat and in the live animal small eyes are present along the mantle margin which

detect changes in light intensity. Many species rest unattached on the sea floor.

Thorny Oysters (Family: Spondylidae) are related to scallops, but the shell is heavier, extended into attractive spines and brightly coloured, and they are only found in tropical waters.

File Shells (Family: Limidae) are small and insignificant shells, but the live animals are beautiful because of the long, colourful tentacles of the mantle edge which hang outside the shell and cannot be retracted. They are related to scallops.

Giant Clams (Family: Tridacnidae) include the largest sea-shells known and need little introduction. All live in the tropical waters of the Indo-Pacific.

Cockles (Family: Cariidae) are shallow burrowers found in all seas. Both valves are strongly convex and when the shell is viewed from either the anterior or posterior end it appears heart-shaped. The shell is solid, the surface usually ribbed and the free edges wavy. Many are edible.

Venus Shells (Family: Veneridae) are a large family distributed throughout the seas of the world. They are shallow burrowers with thick shells and exhibit a great variety of sculptures and colours. The quahog of America belongs to this family.

Tellins (Family: Tellinidae) are fragile shells, usually shiny and delicately coloured and very flat, because they burrow very deeply. The siphon scar (pallial sinus) is deep, indicating that in life the siphons are long; they are detritus feeders.

Otter Shells (Family: Mactridae) are large, elongated and somewhat oval in shape with a deep siphon scar, indicating that the siphons are long and therefore that the animal is a deep burrower.

Jack-knife or Razor Shells (Family: Solenidae) are easily recognized by the long and narrow form of the shell.

Piddocks (Family: Pholadidae) are bivalves with delicate, brittle shells that bore their way into rocks and live in the burrows they make for themselves. The two valves are only loosely attached and gape at the anterior end.

Left
This shows the beautiful inner surface of one valve of the magnificent pen shell, *Pinna nobilis*, which lives in the shallow sandy and muddy waters of the Mediterranean. This bivalve lives in the sandy mud with its anterior or pointed end downwards, retaining its position by attaching byssus threads to buried stones. These threads, which are fine and silky, were at one time used to make small items of dress such as gloves, but as one pen shell yields only one gram of byssus threads the industry was too expensive to survive. The central groove or sulcus and the attractive bluish-grey mother-of-pearl towards the narrow end are typical of this largest species of pen shell, which may be 40 cm long.

Below centre
The radiating pinkish-red bands identify this as the virgate tellin, *Tellina virgata*, of the Indo-Pacific, a species which may be 6 cm in length. The valves are considerably flattened, an indication that it burrows deeply; it lives in the sand, and because it is a detritus feeder it has two long, narrow separate siphons.

Below
Although this lovely bivalve is commonly called a thorny oyster, it is in no way related to the true oysters, but is actually allied to the scallops. The characteristic features which make these handsome shells popular with collectors are the rich colours and the long spines on the ribs of the valves. While they are alive thorny oysters do not look so attractive because they become thickly encrusted with various marine growths as they live attached to rocks in shallow waters down to a depth of 30 metres. The valves are solid and the inner surface porcellaneous. This is the Pacific thorny oyster, *Spondylus princeps*, which is found along the west coast of America from California to Panama.

Above
This exquisite frilled venus, *Callanaitis disjecta*, is also called the wedding-cake venus and once seen is not easily forgotten. It inhabits sandy mudbanks along the Australian coast from New South Wales to South Australia, and it may be 6 cm long.

This page
File shells, like scallops, are free and capable of swimming, though rather more feebly. They are particularly attractive bivalves with long, trailing tentacles that fringe the mantle margin. These tentacles cannot be completely withdrawn within the shell, so for protection file shells construct a type of nest from a network of byssus threads, set amongst the stones, gravel and weeds of the shallow water. They rest within this protective barrier, feeding on plankton filtered from the indrawn water. File shells can open their valves much wider than most other bivalves, as can be seen in the gaping file shell, *Lima hians*, *left* which lives in the area between low water and a depth of 100 metres in the waters of the Mediterranean and the northeastern Atlantic, extending as far north as the Orkney Islands. The shell rarely exceeds a length of 2.5 cm. Above is the Indian Ocean species, *Lima rotundata*, which may be 4.5 cm long.

45

Right
This bear's paw clam shows the solid, porcellaneous nature of the shells of the large bivalves of the Indo-Pacific. The hardness of the shell led to the use of giant clam shells for making tools such as mallets and hoes; some of the largest valves were used as baptismal fonts, washbasins and bird baths.

Below
This delicately sculptured bivalve is the giant frilly clam, *Tridacna maxima*, but it is small in comparison with *Tridacna gigas*, as it only grows to a length of 35.3 cm. It too inhabits coral reefs throughout the Indo-Pacific, but is attached to the substratum by a byssus.

Bottom
This is the inner surface of the right valve of a bivalve mollusc showing the scars left by various parts of the living animal. The two similar shaped scars on either side are

the adductor muscle scars; on the left is the scar of the anterior adductor and the scar on the right is that of the posterior adductor. The line running from the anterior adductor to the posterior of the shell and parallel to its outer edge shows where the right mantle lobe was attached; scientists call it the pallial line. The indentation in this line just before it joins the posterior adductor is called the pallial sinus; this shows where the siphons entered the shell. In bivalves with no siphons the pallial line continues parallel to the edge until it reaches the posterior adductor scar. The shape and position of these scars are regularly used in identification. This specimen is a carpet shell and can be recognized as the species known as a pullet carpet, *Venerupis pullastra* .

Right
This giant clam, *Tridacna gigas*, is growing amongst coral in shallow water and its attractive fleshy mantle lobes can be seen exposed between the two valves. This species is the largest known bivalve, the record being 137 cm. The giant clams are basically suspension feeders which filter plankton from the sea water, but they have a second source of food and in fact form food in their own tissues. Zooxanthellae, minute unicellular algae, live in the thick edges of the mantle lobes where they are exposed to sufficient light for their needs. When required as food these zooxanthellae are passed to the digestive gland of the clam. This species is unattached, the weight of the shell itself keeping it in position. It inhabits coral reefs throughout the Indo-Pacific.

Previous pages
Stranded along the driftline after a storm are these otter shells, *Lutraria lutraria*, which normally live offshore to a depth of 90 metres buried in sand or sandy mud. The edges of these shells were damaged when they were tossed ashore and some have died with their joined siphons partially extended. The brown periostracum still covers parts of the shells. This species can be 12.5 cm long and is found from the coasts of the British Isles to the Mediterranean. Similar species occur in other temperate waters.

Left
This beautifully sculptured costate cockle, *Cardium costatum*, comes from West Africa. Notice how the wide, raised ribs and the deep grooves are arranged so that when the valves are closed a groove in one valve corresponds with a rib in the other. Each rib bears a spinous extension which is hollow on the inner surface, and here alternate solid and hollow spines can be seen around the margin of the closed valves. This species may grow to a size of 10 cm.

Above
This beautiful great scallop, *Pecten maximus*, lives on the sea floor resting on the rounded right valve with the flat left valve slightly raised. The mantle edge is fringed with delicate tentacles and small eyes occur between them. These are seen here as dark dots along the upper margin. The space between the two lobes of the mantle seen within can be varied to control the inflow and outflow of water. When small, scallops live attached to the substratum by byssus threads; later in life they become free and capable of swimming vigorously flapping the two valves. This species is the edible scallop, which is found in the temperate seas of the northeastern Atlantic and North Sea, and may grow to a length of 15 cm.

Right
This is the delightful heart cockle, *Corculum cardissa*, which is common in the Indo-Pacific, including the northern coast of Australia. It is a delicate shell which must be handled carefully. Each valve is anteriorly posteriorly compressed, making it strongly convex in shape with a ridge along the midline which bears small spines, seen here around the margin of the heart. As in all cockles the valve edges are crenulated and interlock with one another. In this specimen the heart was 4.5 cm long, but a length of 7.5 cm may be reached.

Beautiful varieties

The beauty of seashells depends on their shape, sculpture, size, texture, colour and pattern, and it seems amazing that such attractive structures are produced by rather insignificant invertebrate animals.

The shape and sculpture of a shell depends entirely on the shape of the mantle edge at the time its glands are secreting the shell. For instance, in a spider conch the first-formed whorls near the apex are regularly shaped, so the edge of the mantle is smooth at this stage; with further growth, however, a change occurs, and the mantle edge folds into tabular structures, which means that the shell laid down at this time follows its shape and forms the spines on the outer lip of the aperture. The spines on the venus comb murex are produced in exactly the same way, but they are much thinner and finer. In other species the extensions may be branched, ridged or knobbed. Considering the huge variety of shapes produced, the zoologist is entitled to conjecture what is the function of this sculpturing.

Sharp-pointed spines covering a large area of the shell no doubt protect a mollusc from predators, but not all the variations fall into this category.

Univalves which inhabit the intertidal zones of rocky shores often have to withstand the pounding action of the waves, so their shells are thick, usually with rough, knobbed or ridged surfaces. Shell surfaces within one species may vary considerably depending on the habitat. For instance, common Atlantic dog whelks of the species *Nucella lapillus*, which live in sheltered positions have a much rougher shell than those that inhabit exposed areas, because the latter become smooth through friction as they are rolled along the shore.

Another function of the spines and knobs may well be camouflage. When shells with such complex surfaces become encrusted with marine growths they merge into the surroundings, thus protecting the living molluscs from predators.

Shell variation often occurs within a species according to age. The young shells of cowries have a distinct spire and a normal-shaped aperture, but in the adults the spire is covered by the body whorl and the aperture reduced to a slit bounded by thickened incurved lips. Conches also show this variation with age, the flared lip only being present in the adults. The size of the shell in any one species is dependent on the environment; for normal growth there must be an adequate food supply coupled with water of the correct temperature and salinity.

The shape and sculpture of a shell is related to the habit of the living mollusc. In burrowing bivalves the shell surface is fairly smooth and the valves are flattened to reduce resistance as the shell is drawn through the sand or mud. Also the quieter and deeper the waters in which molluscs live, the thinner and less sculptured the shells.

Some shells have delicate hues and some have elaborate colour patterns, while others are quite drab. Colour depends on the presence of the necessary pigments in the mantle cells and the source of these pigments is presumed to be the food of the mollusc. This suggestion is probably the case when a mollusc feeds on more than one type of prey, but in the flat periwinkle, *Littorina littoralis*, great colour variation occurs even though the individuals feed on the same brown seaweed! Queen scallops also exhibit a wide colour range; as they are filter feeders the diet is likely to be varied, so here is a case where the colour variation may well be related to the food.

The beautiful iridescence of mother-of-pearl is not caused by the presence of pigments, but as we have seen too, is the result of the physical structure of the shell.

Above
The iridescent mother-of-pearl inner surface of abalone shells makes them extremely popular as ornaments and for shell jewellery, so the abalone fishing industries sell the shells as well as the meat. This species has a narrower shell than most and its shape has led to the common name of donkey's or ass's ear. *Haliotis asinia* inhabits the coral reefs of the South Pacific, particularly the Great Barrier Reef, and may grow to a length of 10 cm.

Left
The attractive ornamentation of this coral shell, *Tolema australis*, suggests it is a close relative of the murex shells. In fact, it belongs to a separate family, the Magilidae, and these univalves all live in close association with corals. The various species exhibit a great variety in shell form, but one feature in common is that the animals have no radula; as they are carnivorous, they therefore probably simply suck out the juices from their prey. This species may be 4 cm long and it lives along the southeastern coast of Australia from New South Wales to Victoria.

Left
These delicate, thin tellins, *Tellina tenuis*, compete with queen scallops as the most attractive bivalves to be found from Norway to the Mediterranean. The shells are glossy and brittle and the valves flat, indicating that in life these molluscs burrow deeply. They live in fine sand from the lower shore to a depth of a few metres and as they are detritus feeders, they have long slender siphons. Large specimens may measure 2.5 cm in length. The rose-petal tellin, *Tellina lineata*, which inhabits the waters of Florida and the West Indies, is very similar, and many other beautiful species of the same genus live in other waters of the world.

Right
The ornate sculpture of this fluted clam, *Tridacna squamosa*, makes it one of the most pleasing of the giant clams of the Indo-Pacific. The shell itself is heavy and porcellaneous, but its attraction lies in the broad leaflike scales along the wide ribs and the fluted margins of the valves. It lives on the surface of coral reefs attached by a weak byssus and may grow to a length of 40.8 cm.

Below
These beautiful queen scallops, *Chlamys opercularis*, demonstrate the fantastic colour variation that is possible in the shells of just one species of mollusc. This is one of the most attractive bivalves, found in temperate waters from Norway to the Mediterranean. The young are attached to the substratum by a byssus, but the adults are free and are active swimmers, covering greater distances than any other scallops inhabiting the same area. They live on firm sandy gravel or sandy mud to a depth of about 182 metres, often in large populations. During the last century the larger beds were fished, but although queen scallops can be eaten raw or cooked, they were mainly used for bait. Specimens measuring some 8.5 cm do occur, but generally they are considerably smaller than this. The distinct, raised white lines on some of the shells are the empty limy tubes of polychaete worms.

Right
The flat periwinkle, *Littorina littoralis (obtusata)*, is the most colourful of the periwinkles, ranging from white, yellow, orange, brown and grey to black. It is an intertidal species found on rocky shores where it crawls amongst the fronds of fucoids, brown seaweeds on which it feeds and also deposits its gelatinous egg capsules. The spire is flattened, the body whorl large, the surface smooth and the overall shape oval. The shell is solid and may reach a length of 1.7 cm and breadth of 1.3 cm. The flat periwinkle is common on rocky coasts on both sides of the North Atlantic.

54

Right and far right
These two splendid shells belong to the
same family and exhibit the varied and
extravagant growth of some of the
handsome murex shells. The long,
graceful, sharp-pointed spines of the
venus comb murex, *Murex triremis,
right* must surely ensure that the animal
does not fall victim to a marine predator.
The siphonal canal is very long and
narrow and its two edges nearly meet, but
do not quite achieve it. Large specimens
can be 15 cm long. In comparison the
ramose murex, *Murex ramosus, far right*
is a large, solid shell with a short siphonal
canal, and instead of spines the shell is
ornamented with curved branches, frilly
at the tips. This is one of the largest
species of murex and can be 30 cm long.
As might be anticipated from the complex
sculpturing of these shells, both these
species inhabit the tropical waters of the
Indo-Pacific.
Below
The spines extending from the posterior
region of the valves give this royal comb
venus a beauty all its own. This
extravagant development along the
growth lines is indicative of a warm-water
species. *Hysteroconcha dione* is found
from Texas to the Caribbean and a
similar species from southern California
to Peru. A large specimen may be
4.5 cm long.

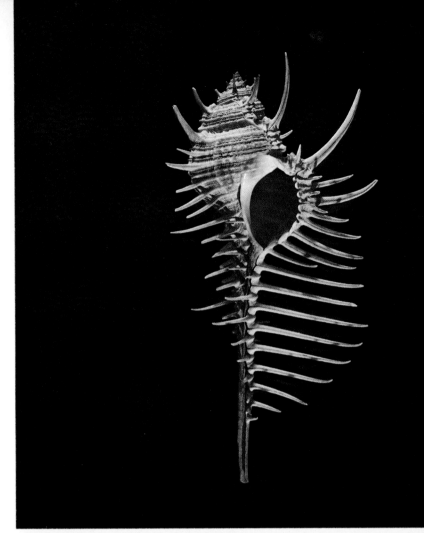

Right
Sometimes a young mollusc does not
exhibit all the characteristics of the
adult and this often poses a problem in
its identification. Here can be seen the
gradual development of the peculiarly
shaped outer lip of the pelican's foot
shell, *Aporrhais pes-pelecani.* This species
buries itself just below the surface in
sandy mud and its range extends from
the North Sea to the Mediterranean.
A similar species, *Aporrhais occidentalis,*
is found along the eastern coast of North
America from Labrador to Carolina.

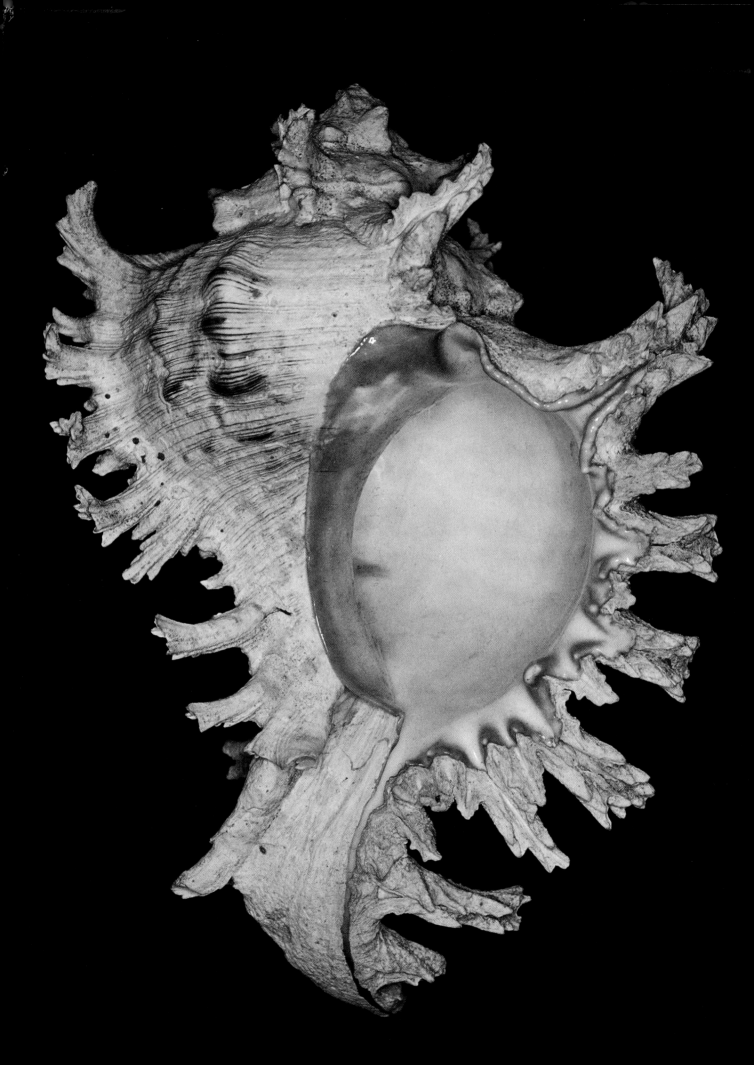

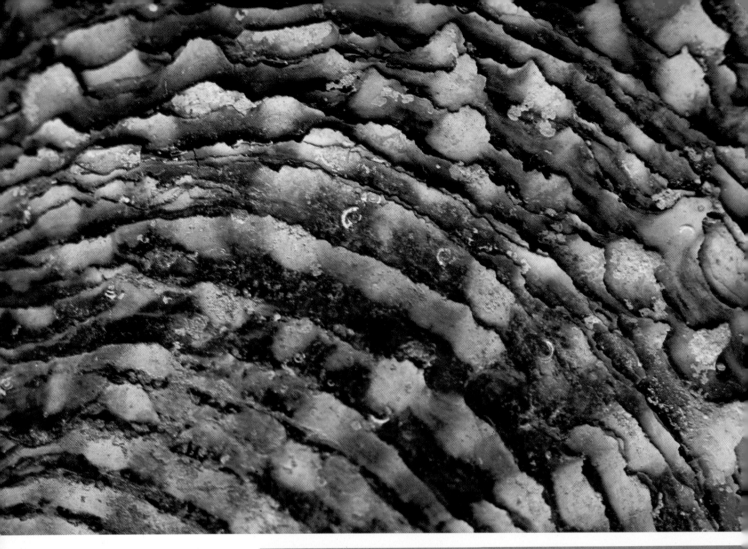

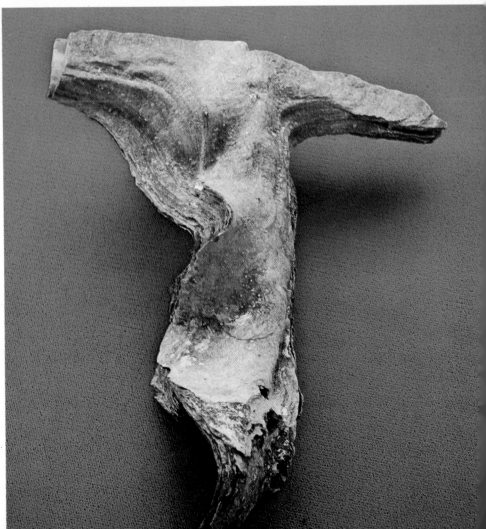

Above

A pattern that somewhat resembles overlapping uneven tiles on a roof is displayed by the outer surface of the pearl oyster, *Pinactada margaritifera.* The lamella represent the concentric growth lines of the shell.

Right

This handsome shell is most unusual in shape and it is easy to imagine that a growth-encrusted specimen brought up from the sea floor could be mistaken for an old hammer. It is almost unbelievable that an animal can live between the two valves of this hammer oyster, *Malleus malleus.* The hinge line is along the top of the T and the one large adductor muscle is situated below this in the central region. The hammer oyster lives attached to the bottom by a byssus, and inhabits the waters of the Indo-Pacific.

Above
Another beautiful and colourful pattern, this time produced by a close-up of the thorny oyster shell, *Spondylus princeps*.
Right
The common Atlantic dog whelk, *Nucella lapillus*, is carnivorous, but limits its prey to two marine creatures, barnacles and mussels. If a specimen feeds on barnacles exclusively the shell is white, but if its food is exclusively mussels the shell is pale brown. The colour banding on this particular shell suggests that throughout its life the animal continuously varied its diet between barnacles and molluscs. This is a common species on rocky shores of the North Sea, the English Channel and both sides of the North Atlantic. In America it is commonly called the Atlantic dogwinkle. Specimens can be 4.5 cm long.

Man and seashells

Man has used seashells in diverse ways from time immemorial;
the succulent flesh as food, the shells as jewellery, ornaments,
utensils, tools, money and religious symbols, and the secretions
of some as dyes and inks.

Today oysters are a universal delicacy and many other
molluscs such as cockles, mussels, quahogs, scallops, winkles,
whelks and abalones are eaten in various parts of the world and
are frequently cultivated for this purpose. Many of the Pacific
species have been a source of food to the islanders throughout
history. Sometimes the flesh is eaten raw, but more usually it is
cooked in some way, as in clam chowder, the popular American
dish made from the quahog clam. Many more shellfish can be
eaten than is generally known; for instance, the razor shells (or
jackknife clams) normally dug up by fishermen for use as bait
are edible and make a tasty meal when cooked correctly.

In early times utensils and tools were made from seashells,
particularly on coral islands where stone was absent. Some shells
were of suitable size and shape for direct use, such as many of
the large volutes or baler shells, which were used frequently as
water carriers, and scallop shells, which are still used as dishes
for holding food.

Early man used shells as currency and this practice continued
until the production of the metal coin, and even after this date
in Africa. The money cowrie, a small cowrie about 2 cm long,
which inhabits the warm tropical oceans of the Indo-Pacific,
came into world-wide use and even in the nineteenth century
some European countries obtained tons of money cowries to
use for barter among the African tribes. Another Indo-Pacific
shell often used as money was the gold-ringer cowrie, and the

American Indians made use of the money tusk, a scaphopod
some 4.5 cm long which lives offshore along the west coast of
America from Alaska to Mexico. The tubular tusk shells were
usually strung together and, of course, a string of perfect shells
was considered far more valuable than one of broken specimens.
The North American Indians also cut and ground beads from
the common quahog clam, drilled them and then strung them
together for use as money. Currency like this in the form of
strings of shell beads was called wampum. Wampum was made
from other shells as well and the value varied accordingly. The
Indians also used shell beads to make wampum belts and in
these belts the beads were strung together in a special way to
convey a message.

Beads cut from shells were used for personal decoration and
as tusk shells are tubular they were simply cut into sections and
threaded on to cord to make necklaces. Complete small shells of
many species made attractive necklaces, as they still do today.
Some of the magnificent helmet shells and large conch shells of
the warm oceans were cut into cameos, and abalones, once they
had been cleaned to expose the iridescent mother-of-pearl, were
used as pendants. In modern times shell jewellery has become a
commercial industry and in all coastal holiday resorts seashells,
either in the form of jewellery or of ornaments, are on display
to attract the tourist.

The mother-of-pearl of many of the larger top shells was the
original source of the pearl button, but the industry has now
declined with the introduction of man-made plastics.

Pearls have always been valued very highly and although
pearls may be found in any bivalve the most beautiful and

perfect are formed in the pearl oysters and the finest in *Pinctada margaritifera*. The Persian Gulf and the northern and north-western coasts of Australia are the principal areas for pearl fishing from this species, but of all the oysters opened only about 2 per cent contain pearls and of these only a few are of a reasonable size. Consequently, real pearls have been extremely expensive to buy, although they retain their value. The last century has seen the growth of a big cultured pearl industry, centred in Japan in which tiny pieces of shell are deliberately inserted between the tissues of the pearl oyster, and then the animal secretes nacreous layers around it, just as in the formation of a natural pearl. Its advantage is that the size of the pearl can be controlled by the amount of time allowed to elapse before the oyster is opened to disgorge its pearl.

Over the centuries the beauty of seashells has been an inspiration in both art and architecture. In Botticelli's famous painting *The Birth of Venus*, Venus is depicted travelling shorewards on a scallop shell.

As symbols shells have played an important role in the life of man. Even today there is one that is familiar to all who travel the motorways of the world, the scallop on the petrol pumps of the Shell Oil Company. Many shells were sacred to primitive tribes. Cowries were a symbol of fertility and often given as bridal gifts. To the Hindus the Indian chank is the most sacred of shells and is used in religious ceremonies. The supposed sound of the sea that is heard when cowrie shells are held close to the ear was thought by some native tribes to be the voice of God and the Polynesians believed that God was actually present in trumpet shells. In Egyptian times shells were used to depict

the eyes in the funeral effigies in which mummies were enclosed and through the centuries shells have been considered as charms against evil spirits. In the Middle Ages the scallop shell was used as a symbol in connection with the crusades to the Holy Land and the inclusion of the scallop shell in heraldic coats of arms may well indicate that a forebear had made such a pilgrimage.

Molluscs belonging to the murex family secrete a pale-coloured fluid which on exposure to light gradually darkens until it becomes purple. This was used as a dye by ancient civilizations.

One relationship between seashells and man which has continued through the ages and is still with us today is the intriguing hobby of shell collecting. It is more exciting and fascinating if one can personally wander along the shores in search of discarded shells washed up on the beach by the tide, but many people find pleasure in building up collections from any possible source, including actual purchase of shells. In Europe a great enthusiasm for shell collecting developed in the fifteenth and sixteenth centuries when trading routes were opened up in previously unknown areas of the world, but it was not until the Victorian era that it reached its peak. The craze for collecting impedimenta has passed in these days of smaller houses and lack of free time, but to search for shells on the shore and to study the animals that live in them remains an enthralling hobby. It is vital, however, that we be discriminate in our collecting or else within a few decades the molluscan populations will be seriously depleted or, in the case of inter-tidal species, even near extinction.

The true beauty of the living animal can only be appreciated

61

Right
This heavy pear-shaped shell with a short
spire, siphonal groove and ridged inner lip
is a shell sacred to the Hindus and is used
extensively in religious ceremonies. A
sinistral specimen is even more highly
valued and supposed to have far greater
powers than this normal dextral form.
This is the Indian chank shell, *Turbinella
(Xancus) pyrum*, which is found only in
the coastal waters of India. The largest
specimens, some 15 cm in length are
carved into bangles, bracelets and
pendants, and may even be used as
trumpets.

Far right
This golden cowrie, *Cypraea aurantium*, is
one of the most valuable cowries and in
the Fiji Islands it is worn by native chiefs
as a badge of office. Shells used in this
way as body ornaments usually have a
small perforation in the side. The golden
cowrie has always been a collector's piece
and although not rare is highly priced
because of its popularity. The animal lives
in caves and holes in the coral reefs of the
Central Pacific at depths from seven to
18 metres, but it has always been most
abundant around the Fiji Islands.
However, now that aqualung divers are
investigating wider areas, the range of the
golden cowrie is proving to be more
extensive.

in its natural environment. We live in a rapidly shrinking world
where jet travel can convey tourists to places that were once
seen only by a few explorers. Unfortunately, once there, the
inexperienced tourist all too often demands souvenirs to remind
him of his holiday in faraway places. This is rapidly creating a
grave situation in many of the rich tropical areas where from
time immemorial molluscan populations have abounded, un-
influenced by man. The small native populations living in a
comparatively primitive state demanded little from their
environment and so the seashells survived, but today the sudden
impact of vast numbers of people collecting and buying seashells
is seriously affecting the balance of the environment. The
souvenir hunter always demands the largest and most attractive
specimen and so the commercial collectors devastate the reefs
by irresponsible gathering. It is possible today to walk along
shores of the Indian Ocean and find not a single shell upon the
beach and only a few in the intertidal pools.

At long last we are slowly becoming aware of man's relationship with his environment, and in the same way that we have
become conscious of pollution we must become conscious of
our depredations on wildlife — and stop them. Of one thing we
may be certain: if seashells are collected at the present un-
controlled rate our children and our children's children will
never again see in natural surroundings the beauty that this
book is endeavouring to portray.

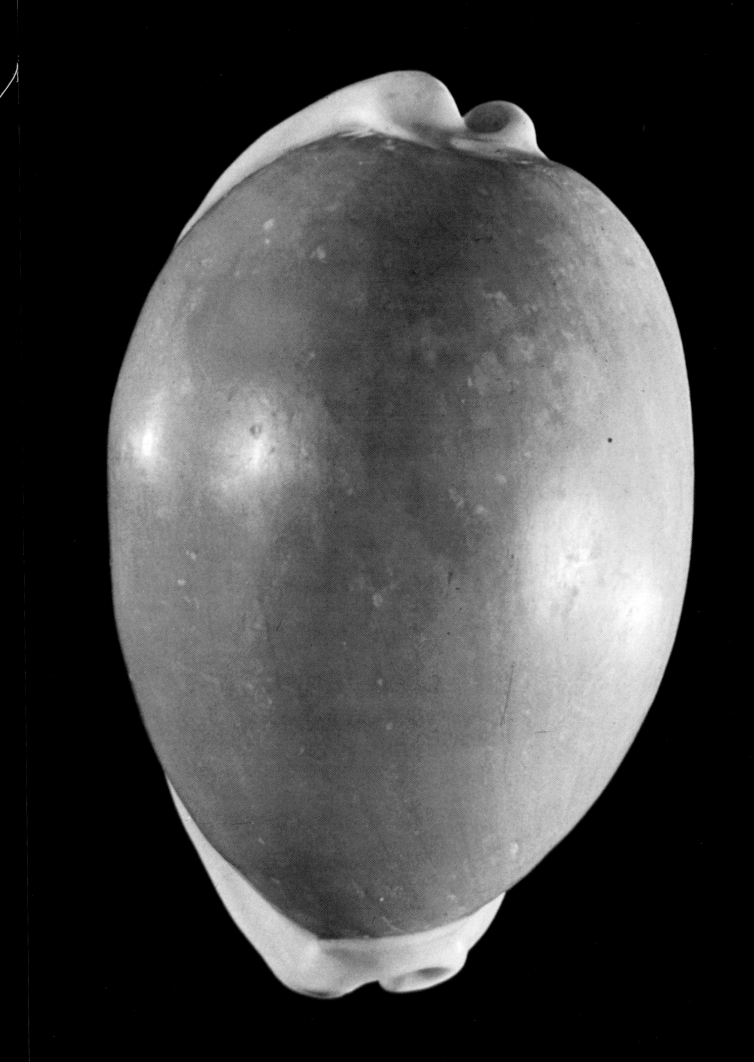

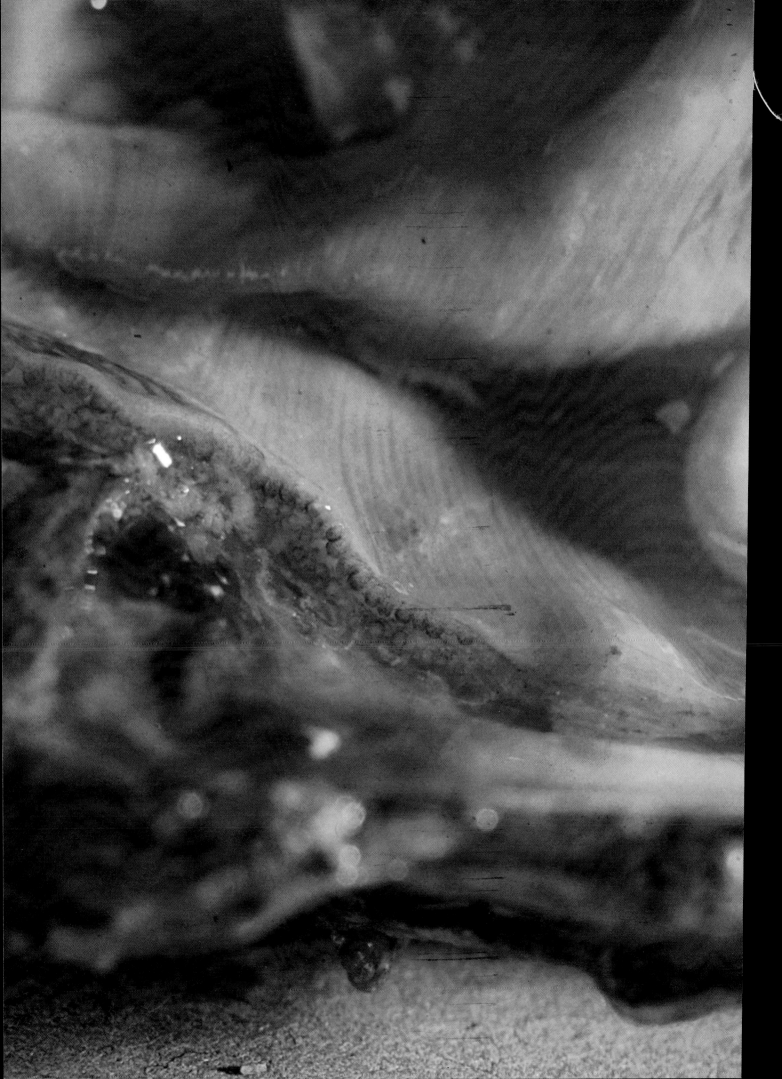

Previous pages
This oyster has been opened and part of the body tissue lifted to expose the pearl *in situ.* This pearl has been produced between the tissue and the mantle and is a perfect sphere, but if a foreign particle becomes lodged between the mantle and the shell the pearl formed will be attached to the shell and is then referred to as a 'blister' pearl. Blister pearls are of little value unless they are large enough to be cut from the shell, but even then they do not equal the value of a perfect pearl.

This page
Melon or baler shells are large volutes with a greatly reduced spire, rounded body whorl and a very large, wide, flaring aperture. These last two features are the reason why natives used the empty shells as water carriers or to bale the water out of their canoes. All species live in tropical seas and the Indian volute, *Melo melo, right* from Southeast Asian waters may reach a length of 20-25 cm. The animals have a large foot but no operculum, and all are carnivores. Hunter's volute, *Cymbiolista hunteri, above* is a smaller species whose maximum size is only about 14 cm. It inhabits deep water off the northern coast of New South Wales, Australia, and in this picture the foot of the animal is extended and the tip of the siphon can just be seen. Even in the live animal the smooth surface and markings of the shell are apparent.

66

This page

Large species of tritons like this were at one time used as trumpets. This was achieved by either removing the tip of the spire or drilling a small round hole in the side of the spire. When the shell is blown into, the sound produced resembles that of a modern cornet, the tone depending on the size of the triton shell. Trumpet tritons are found both in the Caribbean and the Indo-Pacific; this is the Pacific triton, *Charonua tritonis, right* with the orange-pink interior. In comparison this closely related red whelk, *Charonia rubicunda, above* from New South Wales waters, is small; it only reaches a length of 15 cm. Here the shell is encrusted with many marine organisms; notice particularly the large number of barnacles of varying sizes and the limy tubes of polychaete worms.

Right
This abalone, ormer, ear shell or sea ear, as this mollusc is variously called, could easily be mistaken for one half of a bivalve shell; however, as can be seen, a tiny spire is present above the large, flattened body whorl. Notice that the row of holes are open near the free margin but closed towards the spire; as the animal grows and larger perforations are formed, the older ones are sealed on the inner surface. The animal moves sluggishly over rocks, browsing on vegetation, but it also uses its large, flat, muscular foot for clinging tenaciously to rock surfaces. There are some 100 species, many of them gregarious, widely distributed in the warmer waters of the world. Abalone meat is considered a delicacy by many and where the larger species are abundant they are fished commercially. The meat is cleaned and prepared and put on the market fresh, frozen or canned. Such fisheries occur along the west coast of America from southern California to Mexico. This specimen is the black abalone, *Haliotis cracherodi*, which may grow to a length of 15 cm and lives along the coast from Oregon to Lower California.

Far right
Clusters of this common edible periwinkle, *Littorina littorea*, are exposed on the middle shore when the tide recedes, either clinging to a rock as shown here or lying in a gully. In the latter case each member of the cluster has its aperture closed by the tightly fitting operculum to prevent dehydration. The shell colour is drab, but its shape and thickness particularly adapt it for withstanding the pounding of the surf; the animal simply retracts its body, closes the aperture and allows itself to be rolled along by the tide. The spire is pointed, though it tends to become worn down in older specimens and the body whorl is large. The shell can grow to a length of 3 cm. This species lives on both sides of the Atlantic and is used as a food in Europe. However, it is a somewhat tiresome and intricate process to obtain the flesh; after cooking a pin is used to untwist the animal from the columella.

Right
The yellow ring around this beautifully polished greyish-white cowrie identifies it as the gold-ringer, *Cypraea annulus.* From early times this cowrie was popular with the natives for decorative purposes and also as legal tender. It grows to about 2.5 cm in length and is common throughout the Indo-Pacific. It inhabits shallow tidal pools and shallow water under stones and amongst vegetation.

These are money cowries, *Cypraea moneta*, which were used extensively as money by primitive man. They are well suited for this purpose as the shell is very solid and of a size suitable for handling. These are all about 1.8 cm, but the species may grow to some 3.0 cm. Instead of having the usual smooth appearance of cowries, the dorsal surface is rather knobbly. They are common in shallow water over the entire area of the Indo-Pacific.

Below right
This common or smooth spider conch, *Lambis lambis*, is one of the most abundant univalves in many of the shallow-water areas of the Indo-Pacific. Consequently it has long been used as a nutritious food by many of the island communities, being eaten raw or cooked. In Ceylon, Tamil fishermen roast the animal in the shell before eating it. In this live specimen the tip of the foot can just be seen protruding from the aperture. This species is identified by the six slender spines, the fairly short siphonal canal and the distinct stromboid notch between the sixth spine and the siphonal canal; also the lips and aperture are smooth and shiny. This species varies considerably in colour and it may grow to a length of 20 cm.

Right
Easily recognized as a top shell by its pyramidal shape and flattened base, this large, heavy species with a thick nacreous layer was used to manufacture pearl buttons. After removal of the attractively patterned outer surface the buttons were cut from the shell following along the whorls, giving buttons of several sizes from one shell – the largest from the body whorl. This is the commercial top shell, *Trochus niloticus*, which may grow to a height of 12.5 cm. It is a vegetarian and therefore lives in shallow waters where plant life is plentiful; as would be expected from its size and colour, it is a tropical-water species. Its range extends from the Indian Ocean to Samoa and from Queensland to Japan. Between the two world wars it was fished so extensively that it was almost in danger of extinction, but with reduced fishing during the war years it recovered and is out of danger now that man-made plastics are used for buttons.

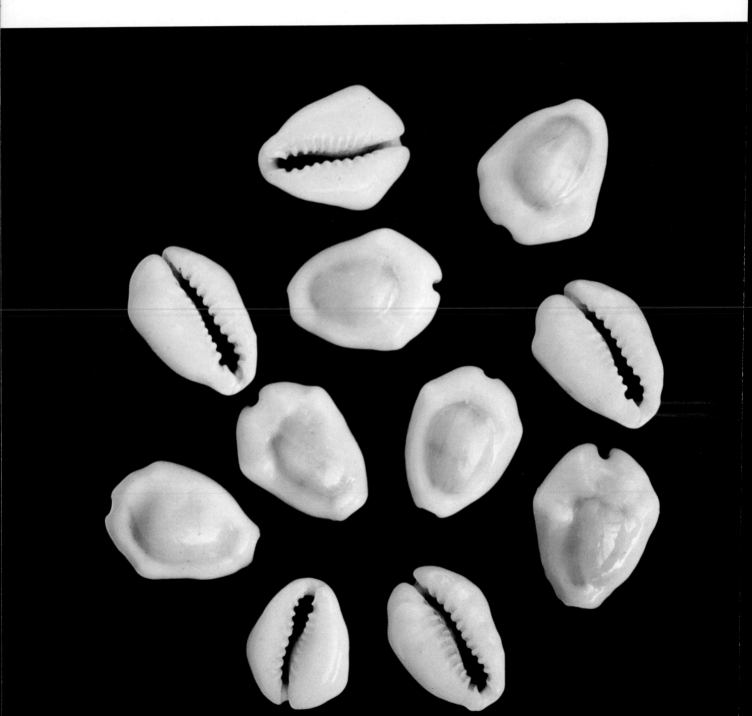

Acknowledgments

The publishers would like to thank the
following individuals and organizations
for their kind permission to reproduce the
pictures in this book:

Anthony Bannister, NHPA 13, 29, 33 top,
45 top

J. M. Clayton, NHPA 4-11, 12 top, 14 left,
15-23, 26-28, 30-32, 33 bottom, 34,
35 bottom, 38-44, 45 bottom, 46, 48-9,

50 bottom, 51-2, 53 top, 54-6, 58-60,
62-3, 66 bottom, 67 bottom, 68-9, 70,
71 top

Leslie Jackman, NHPA 12 bottom, 24-25,
50 top, 71 bottom

Spectrum Colour Library 64-65

Walter Deas 14 top and bottom, 36-37,
47, 53 bottom, 57, 61, 66 top, 67 top

A GASTROPOD SHELL

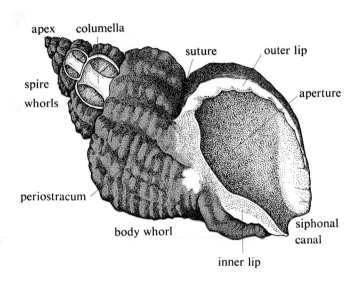

apex
columella
suture
outer lip
spire
whorls
aperture
periostracum
body whorl
siphonal canal
inner lip

A CONCH SHELL

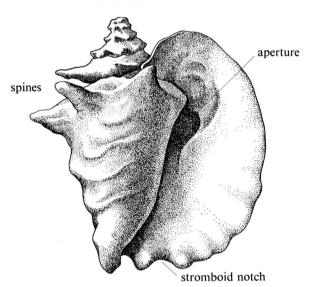

aperture
spines
stromboid notch

A TYPICAL BIVALVE

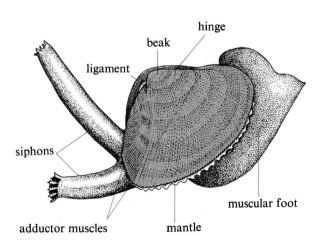

hinge
beak
ligament
siphons
adductor muscles
mantle
muscular foot

A TYPICAL GASTROPOD

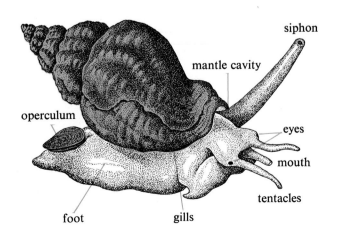

siphon
mantle cavity
operculum
eyes
mouth
tentacles
foot
gills